# GENTLEMEN'S GUIDE to *flirting*

DAVID SHARPE

ISBN: 978-1-7367984-0-9 (print)



For information contact: gentsguidetoflirting@gmail.com

Do it for yourself.

Do it for those who love you and rely on you.

Do it for the family that you envision building.

# CONTENTS

EDUCATION
CAREER
INTIMACY
RELATIONSHIPS
GIVING
BACK
YOU
STARTING A FAMILY
BUSINESS
GOALS

# PART 1

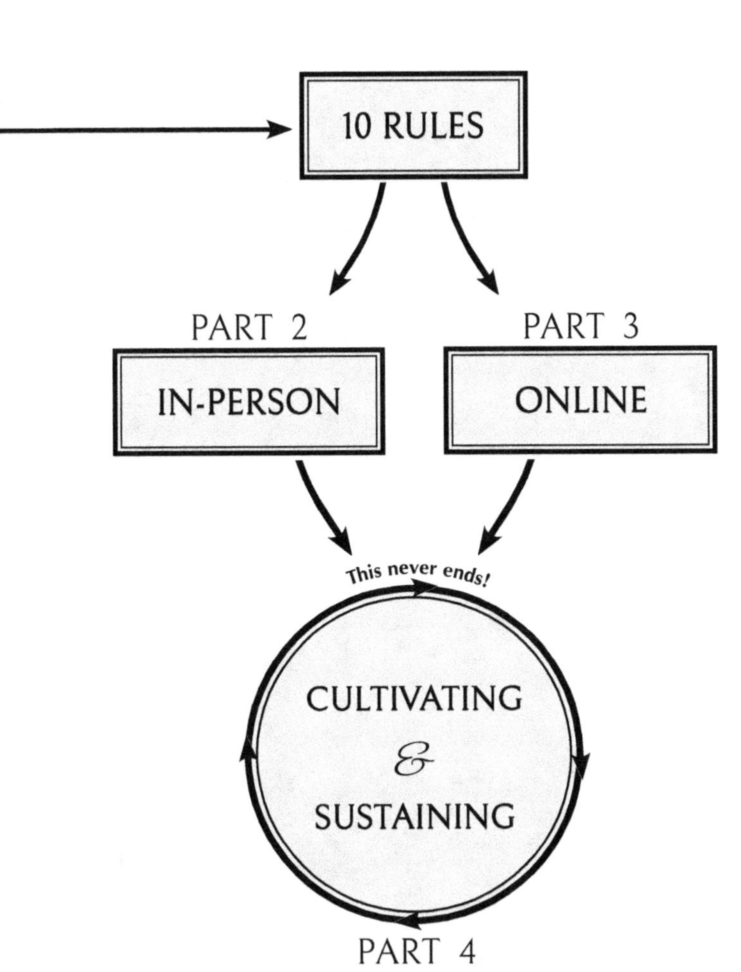
10 RULES
PART 2
IN-PERSON
PART 3
ONLINE
This never ends!
CULTIVATING
&
SUSTAINING
PART 4

# INTRODUCTION

THIS IS NOT A BOOK FOR PICKUP ARTISTS, SCAMMERS, OR PLAYERS. The mindset and approaches described here are more effective for boldly meeting and connecting with ladies in high-quality ways, while being respectful of them and having great fun at the same time. This book is for well-intentioned, genuine, and serious gentlemen who want to improve their confidence naturally and add powerful and life-changing communication and interpersonal skills to their toolbox. Guys without these tools are at a serious disadvantage. Don't let that be you.

This book's purpose is to help men become better at one of the most fun and rewarding life skills you can have: flirting.

*Why flirt?* You can flirt to meet an interesting new person, to express your genuine interest in them, to learn about them, or to begin the process of knowing if someone is a potential match for you. You can also flirt to make someone feel special, valued, and appreciated regardless of how long you have known them.

*How you flirt matters.* There aren't any magic words or clever tactics that work every time, but there is a mindset and a process which makes meeting and connecting with the right woman for you easier. You need to be confident in yourself, knowing you have much to offer. Confidence is crucial, and we will explore that first.

As for the lady, we will cover approaches she will like and feel comfortable with, which build her up as a person, and which both of you will enjoy experiencing together as you work toward determining if she is a potential match for you.

How are we going to get there? Here is the process:

**Part 1**—*Planning and Preparation:* Get yourself and your mindset right. Develop the type of natural self-confidence that makes it easier to approach women. Know what you want. Define precisely what qualities you are looking for in a woman—the ones *she* must have for you *both* to have the best chance at long-term happiness. Lastly, we define our rules of conduct for this entire process.

**Part 2**—*Meeting in Person:* Next, we move to the thought process and mechanics of confidently approaching and meeting women in person. We will cover effective ways to do this and what to avoid. This part is densely packed with modern, field-tested, and ready-to-use examples.

**Part 3**—*Meeting Online:* Meeting women using the internet sounds like it should be easy, but many men find that isn't the case, so we need an entire section for this subject. Toxic behavior on dating sites turns many ladies off. Many women find their inboxes full of unwanted messages, which crowds out the genuine interest from good guys like you. Here, we will use principles from Part 1 to set up your profile and to provide effective methods for reaching out to and connecting with ladies of interest in a confident, safe, productive, and fun way. Loads of practical and reusable real-world examples are provided.

**Part 4**—*Cultivating and Sustaining:* You've met someone. Now you will invest more time to get to know her even better. You need to use the first few dates to see if she is right for you. Practical guidance to help you through these conversations is provided with many examples that will "wow" her and keep her laughing, engaged, and interested. This is where you will show her who you really are—someone she can rely upon; someone she, her family, and her friends will value having in their lives; a strong asset for any future family you might choose to have together; and someone your children will look up to with their hearts full of pride.

**Part 5:** Here we have a toolbox of useful expressions to help you when you are at a loss for words or in need of a cute expression to spice up a conversation. We conclude with a reminder of our Ten Rules, plus some helpful links.

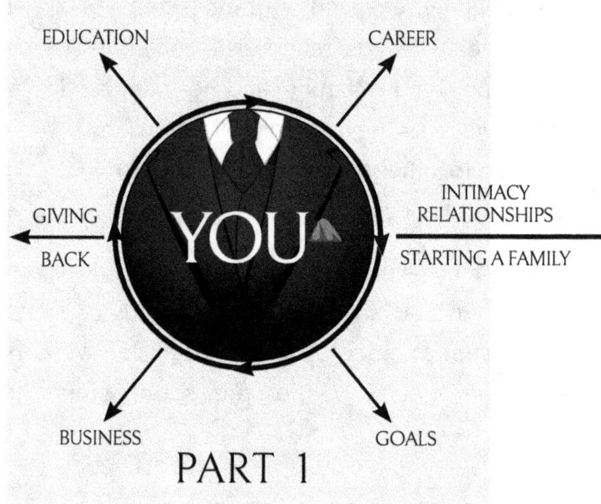
EDUCATION
CAREER
INTIMACY
RELATIONSHIPS
GIVING
BACK
YOU
STARTING A FAMILY
BUSINESS
GOALS
PART 1

*you are here*

# Part 1.
# PLANNING & PREPARATION

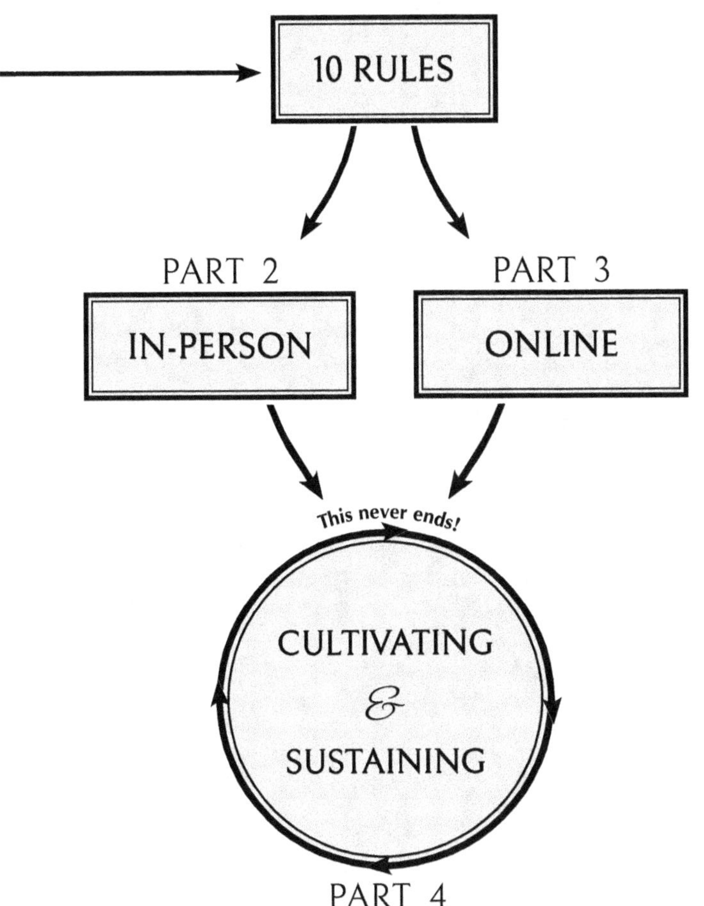

## Your Goal

One of the keys to enduring happiness and satisfaction in life is finding the right woman for you—one who matches what you are looking for in terms of companionship or starting a family. Conversely, one of the surest paths to soul-crushing misery is to end up with the wrong person. To avoid problems, you first need to know what you are looking for, and then not accept less.

There are millions of men out there trapped in unhappy marriages and relationships because they never took the time to really think through what they truly needed in a woman. Some men get laser-focused on a "10" appearance-wise, which later morphs into a daily nightmare for both parties due to a lack of basic compatibility. Some men settle too early in their search for a lady, ending up with someone who only meets a small percentage of what they truly need. In time, these men realize they have made a mistake. Don't let that be you. Much of your long-term happiness in life could depend on your choice.

There are millions of good women out there who are looking for good men. They just need a little help meeting someone like you. Not every woman you will encounter will be a suitable candidate for you, which is okay. You will meet many women using the methods in this book—perhaps too many. For this process to work, you will need to screen candidates.

## Knowing What You Want

What are you looking for? Although this is a book about effective flirting, think about *why* you are doing this. You are approaching these ladies to meet the greatest and best among them. You need to accurately define what that is in your own terms, so you recognize these traits when you see them. Without this, you might let an opportunity to connect with someone great pass you by.

What constitutes or defines the right woman isn't the same for every man. Some men value a woman who is family-oriented, or of a certain religious faith, or one who maintains a healthy lifestyle, or is an artsy free spirit.

> Having a plan and thoroughly thinking through your approach could be one of the most important exercises you go through in your life—it could be one of the keys to your future happiness. This level of preparation will also increase your confidence. If you get this wrong or skip this step, it can be one of the most costly, stressful, and personally damaging mistakes you can make.

We are going to create a compatibility assessment scorecard, meaning a list of the qualities you are looking for and value in a match, and weight the priority of each. You, of course, define which desired qualities go in your list, and what a maximum rating is for each. Perfection is a total score of 100. You will create one of these compatibility assessments for each lady you are considering. Then, as you learn about each one, you will fill out her individual assessment scorecard accordingly.

When done thoughtfully, honestly, and carefully, this process will help you identify what is most important to you in a relationship. If you take a disciplined and thorough approach to this, it should help lower the chances of bad decisions and experiences when it comes to meeting and connecting with the right woman for you.

Yes, this is a scorecard. As cold and clinical as that sounds, it will help you to organize your thoughts and keep your sights on what matters most as you progress through the meeting, screening, and dating process.

> As tempting as it might be, put absolutely nothing about any woman's face, figure, hair, eye color, or anything else about her physical appearance in your compatibility assessment worksheets. Some screening for appearance will come naturally. Trust me. Focus on everything important to you beyond her appearance in your compatibility assessment.

One of the wonderful and magical things about women is that when you find the right one for you, she will look better and better as time progresses, no matter how attractive she was when you first met her. These compatibility assessment scores will be the best predictors of your future happiness with her.

The process of getting to know a woman doesn't have to take a long time. It can take hours, or days, or months. Take your time and get this part of the process right. It could change the course of your life.

To be clear, you are assigning each candidate lady a match score. You are not judging her. This process is to help you make better decisions on who to invest more time with and who to pass on.

Never, ever tell her you are doing this! No one wants to feel like they are being judged.

You must have your finalized list of desired traits and qualities in mind with *every* approach and interaction with a lady. In your conversations and interactions with her, ask questions to find out what you need to know about her based on your goals. Answering some might require you to observe how she reacts to things and behaves in different circumstances while you are spending time together.

> Don't turn this learning and discovery process into an interrogation. No one likes that. Be cool and patient and thoughtfully work in your questions when openings occur.

The tables below cover many possible points to consider for inclusion in your compatibility assessments. Of course, add or remove as needed. For your convenience, this book's website has assessment templates in digital form at *https://gentlemensguidetoflirting.com/assessment-creator.html*.

| HOW DOES SHE ACT AND TREAT YOU? |
| --- |
| Does she make herself available to you the right amount of time (not too little or too much) for dates and conversation? |
| Is she too emotional? Too cold? |
| Is she unreliable or dependable? Late or punctual? |
| Is she too jealous or insecure, not letting you have female friends? |
| Regarding sex and affection, is there too little or too much? |
| Is she kind and thoughtful? |
| She is passionate about (fill in cause/hobby/idea). |

| Does she expect you to spend too much money? |
| --- |
| Is she a good person to live with? |
| Does she want to start a family? Will she be a good mother? |
| How much time does she expect you to spend together? Will you be together all the time or is she less needy regarding how much time you need to spend with her? |
| Does she embarrass, attack, or belittle you? |
| Does she respect you as a person and a man? |
| Is she too controlling or overbearing? |

| COMMUNICATIONS |
| --- |
| Is she a good listener, or does she not listen? |
| Does she talk too much or too little? |
| Does she interrupt you while you're speaking?<br>Is she disrespectful of your opinions? |
| Can she talk through problems, bringing issues up in a constructive way? Is she open to resolution or compromise? |
| Is she articulate, expressing herself intelligently? |
| Does she complain or criticize too much? |
| Does she swear or use vulgar language too much? |

| HOW DOES SHE TREAT OTHERS? |
|---|
| Is she respectful of other people? |
| Is she mean-spirited or hateful? |
| Does she complain too much? |
| How does she treat waitstaff, people in stores, cleaning people, and service people? |
| How does she treat children? |
| How does she treat the elderly? |
| Is she giving and charitable, or is she selfish? |
| How will your most cherished friends, and the people in your family whose opinions and views you value the most, get along with her? Will these social interactions go well? Will those close to you like her? |

| ABOUT HER CURRENT SITUATION |
| --- |
| Does she have children now? |
| Does she have the same goals as you regarding having children (timing, number, when to start)? |
| Is she lazy or sloppy about housework or cleaning in the home? |
| Is she okay with money and finances? Does she spend too much money or too little? |
| Do you like her family? Will they be a problem in any way, or are they great people? Does she have a strong family background? Does she have strong ties to her family? |
| Does she like to travel, or does she prefer to stay at home? |
| Does she smoke, drink, do drugs, or have any substance abuse issues? |
| Does she have a healthy lifestyle? |

| Does she have good table manners and generally practice good etiquette? |
| --- |
| Is she active with a fit lifestyle? Is there an acceptable adventure-to-homebody ratio? |
| What is her financial situation? Does she have a lot of credit card, student loan, or other debt? Does she have a gambling problem or a worrisome credit score? |
| How does she handle stress? Is it medication, alcohol, outbursts, depression? |
| Does she have a good sense of humor? |
| Does she have a good sense of style and good hygiene? |
| Does she have a love of life, vivaciousness, energy, curiosity? |
| Is she organized and dependable, or is she unreliable? |
| Is she caring, selfless? |

| Is she well-educated (what level)? |
| --- |
| Are her religious beliefs compatible with yours? |
| What is the quality of her friends? Does she have many close friends? |
| Does she like pets, especially your pets and animals? |
| Are your political beliefs or affiliations compatible? |
| Are your social beliefs or affiliations compatible? |
| Does she make too many bad major decisions? |
| Does she keep bad company, or have problematic family or friends? |

Here is an example of what a completed scorecard might look like:

| QUALITY | WEIGHT | SCORE |
|---|---|---|
| Is she kind and thoughtful? | 5 | 5 |
| Does she smoke, drink, do drugs, or have any substance abuse issues? | 10 | 5 |
| Is she well-educated (what level)? | 5 | 3 |
| How will your most cherished friends and the people in your family, whose opinions and views you value the most, get along with her? Will they like her? | 20 | 15 |
| Does she have a love of life? Is she vivacious, energetic? | 5 | 5 |
| How does she treat children? | 5 | 5 |
| Is she okay with money and finances? Does she spend too much money or too little? | 20 | 10 |
| Does she expect you to spend too much money? | 5 | 5 |
| Is she a good person to live with? | 20 | 15 |
| How is her sense of humor? | 5 | 5 |
| **TOTAL:** | **100** | **73** |

What constitutes an acceptable score is entirely up to how you do the judging. If you meet 20 women this year, and 19 of them fall into a range of 20–40% out of 100, and one gets a 92%, that might be telling you something. If you judge harshly, it might be impossible for even the best woman to hit 100%. If you judge too easily, it might be hard to tell the best woman apart from the others when scores are grouped too close to hers in the 80–100% range.

You can fine-tune how you score as you gain experience, further refine your definition of what you are looking for over time, and become more comfortable with this process. Be calm and patient. It will come to you in time. You'll know quality when you see it.

It's important to spread these questions out over time as you work toward getting to know her. This isn't an interview or interrogation. Ask a question and then actively and carefully listen to her. Having this list in mind also helps to keep the conversation flowing on your dates.

Don't rush it. Your tactfully and politely delivered screening questions should make her feel that you are interested in her as a person. She is smart and will figure out what you are doing, and that is okay.

And remember, her meeting your compatibility assessment criteria is not just a one-time thing for the initial screening part of the process—it is a requirement for the entire duration of your relationship.

> No matter what, don't ever lose sight of what you are looking for. Your lifelong happiness is crucial.

## Common Pitfalls and Problems

Before we talk about flirting "Do's," we need to talk about some "Don't's." We need to talk about, for lack of a better term, "creepy" guy behavior.

Maybe you have heard someone refer to a person, place, or situation as being "creepy?" At its core, creepiness is a perception of something or someone being a threat. When you are approaching a woman, even with the purest and noblest of intentions, it is easy to make a mistake and be perceived by her as creepy, scary, or a threat to her safety. You want to avoid that perception at all costs.

> How can you avoid seeming "creepy" to women? Basically, make sure your actions and words will most likely be interpreted as follows: 1) You are interested in her for herself, not only for sex; and 2) You are not a threat. She can feel safe around you always, and under all circumstances.

Here are some things to be mindful of and to avoid doing:

- ✗ Don't stare at her. No one wants someone looking at them intently for five minutes at a bar or at the grocery store. I know it isn't always easy to work up the nerve to meet someone new, but do not stare at her while you are coming up with a plan for your approach. A little pre-approach eye contact is okay, especially with a friendly smile and a hello. An honest smile can help her feel comfortable with you, and to relax. Don't underestimate the power of a genuine smile throughout this entire meeting, dating, and relationship process.
- ✗ Don't approach her from behind. She needs to know you are there. You don't want to startle her. She should be able to see you walking toward her, and you should be smiling pleasantly, looking friendly and non-threatening while doing so.
- ✗ Whether standing or seated while having a conversation, don't position yourself in a way that blocks her from being able to move around freely or inhibits her ability to walk away if she feels the need to leave. Don't box her in or trap her in place. For example, if there is a wall, table, or any other type of barrier nearby, make sure that, if anyone's freedom of movement is impeded, it is yours. If she isn't interested or open to the approach, she might feel the need to move away or increase the distance between the two of you. Always ensure she doesn't feel physically trapped or blocked.
- ✗ Don't stand or move too close to her when speaking. Be mindful of her physical cues and body language during your interaction. If she is backing away, allow for more distance between the two of you and adjust what you are doing to help her feel safer and at ease.

- ✗ Don't compliment her too much, and don't rave about how beautiful she is. A nice compliment can be used as an effective ice breaker, but too many compliments can make her feel uncomfortable, question your motives for approaching her, and possibly not trust you. It is okay to tell her how pretty she is in some light, appropriate, and maybe funny way, but move on to another topic or item quickly. That will help take the pressure off her and understand that you are interested in more than just the way she looks.
- ✗ Don't touch her too much, and be careful where you touch her. On your initial approach, don't touch her at all. Later in the conversation, if the moment is right, it might be okay to touch her briefly on maybe the upper arm or hand to make a joke or a point for just a second. Read her body language when you do to see if she draws away from your touch. If she does, don't do it again until you have invested more time and she is showing signs that she trusts you more.
- ✗ Be confident, bold, and brave, but not to the point where she is concerned about her safety.

> Her guard may be up from her own life experience, coupled with the collective wisdom that has been handed down to her from countless generations of women. Your task is to get her to <u>want</u> to lower her defenses, not break through them or trick her. You want her to trust you, so be trustworthy.

Here are some body language cues that may mean she is feeling uncomfortable:

- ✗ She looks away. She turns away or angles her body away from yours. She takes a step or two away from you.
- ✗ If you are both seated, she might lean away from you or otherwise increase the distance between the two of you.
- ✗ She is not listening, smiling, or laughing, or is generally not participating in the conversation.
- ✗ She isn't making eye contact with you.
- ✗ She isn't smiling at all when it would ordinarily be appropriate, or she is frowning or showing some other facial expressions indicating disinterest or discomfort with the situation.
- ✗ Her tone of voice sounds distressed.
- ✗ She fidgets with something, like a cell phone.

Here are some body language signs indicating interest:

- ✓ She makes frequent, friendly eye contact.
- ✓ She is engaged in the conversation.
- ✓ She smiles and laughs at moments that feel right.
- ✓ She maintains an appropriately close physical distance between the two of you. If it is noisy, she leans in closer to hear you.

- ✓ She initiates touching with you from time to time. She doesn't pull back, cringe, or recoil when you touch her.
- ✓ She engages in the conversation and asks questions about you (name, background, occupation, age, family, etc.).
- ✓ She leads or continues the conversation herself.
- ✓ She actively listens and processes what you are saying (likely comparing you to her own internal scorecard criteria for men).
- ✓ She flirts back.

> You are the interesting, fun, reliable, confident and high-quality guy she is looking for—she just doesn't know it yet. Don't miss an opportunity by failing to pay attention to how she is reacting, what her body language is telling you, and what she is saying.

## Proceeding with Confidence

Let's talk about confidence and mindset. Having the desire, a plan, and your compatibility assessment prepared won't matter if you don't have the confidence to proceed or take action. You must project confidence and have the right mindset. I want you to embody that naturally. Note that I did not say "act" confident—I want you to be genuinely confident.

Let's clarify a few things first:

1. It doesn't matter what you look like. Most women don't care if the *right* guy is fat, short, tall, skinny, bald, old, young, or whatever else you think is holding you back. Sure, being handsome might add a few percentage points in her eyes, but looks aren't enough for her for many of the same reasons we omitted her appearance from our compatibility assessment earlier.
2. Do you need to be able to do 100 push-ups? No.
3. Do you need to be able to do 100 sit-ups? No.
4. Do you need to look like a model or movie star? No.

She does want you to be confident, interesting, responsible, trustworthy, and cool. She wants you to be active and ambitious. She wants to feel safe with you. She wants depth of character.

You will be cool and interesting to her because of your mindset. Why? Every day you wake up and work toward your goals. Every day you stack wins toward those goals and continuously improve yourself. You do that to be as valuable as possible to yourself, your family, and everyone else you care about. You are the type of person she wants to build a life and create a family with.

Visually, what I am proposing is shown above. This is the left-most part of the diagram that appears at the beginning of Parts 1 through 4. Starting from the center, you are continuously improving yourself every day. Every day you get up and relentlessly work toward your goals step-by-step. That is what I refer to as stacking wins. Much of your effort goes toward achieving your goals around health and wellness, your career, your education, your business, and your financial success. Whenever you decide you want to pursue a relationship, get married, or start a family, then the arrow to the right kicks in. That arrow to the right flows into the other parts of this book, meaning meeting great women online or in-person in a manner aligned with the Ten Rules. Then, when you have found the right person per what your compatibility assessment and heart are telling you, progressing to a relationship and beyond.

Exploring this book and reaching out to her are part of that process. How you conduct yourself and carry yourself will draw people to you. She will feel your energy.

I'm not talking about false confidence or acting. If you are a long-haired gamer, act like it's the best thing in the world for her to be with a dashing, modern, and technology-savvy guy. If you are a divorced middle-aged man with two children, act like it's the best thing in the world for her to be with an experienced father with two wonderful children. If you are a single, never-married man in his twenties or thirties, act like it's the best thing in the world for her to be with a prime candidate like you who is full of potential. She wants to be with someone she feels safe with, who will be a good provider, and who is confident, fun, and cool. That's you! You should make your good points sound like the greatest thing on Earth, and act like women should be clamoring to be with a guy like you. That should be your attitude.

What are your sources of confidence? Let's go deeper:

1. You are a good person at your core. You know you have good things to offer. You have a plan, are serious, and aren't wasting her time. You know that, if things work out between you, it will make her life better.

2. You know that even her most protective family and friends will like you. Her parents will welcome you. She, and they, can trust you. You would be an asset to all of them.

3. You are the type of person she can build a life with—and raise a family with, if that is what you both want. You are the type of man your children will be proud of.

4. One of your superpowers is that you approach women with the mindset that you already know them, like she has been a close friend for years. Close your eyes and envision that. What tone would you use with such a person? Would you genuinely smile at the sight of her? Would you be totally comfortable with her? You would be perfectly at ease, confident, and respectful. You want her to laugh and be happy. This mind trick is one of my great secrets to confidence. In Parts 2 and 3, you will see many examples of how well this works.

**Life Priorities**

It is important to have your life priorities straight. This concept is much broader than just flirting and dating. Having yourself together and being on a good trajectory in life will do wonders for your confidence and for how people perceive and treat you. This is a lifelong process. For maximum happiness, I suggest the following priority order for you:

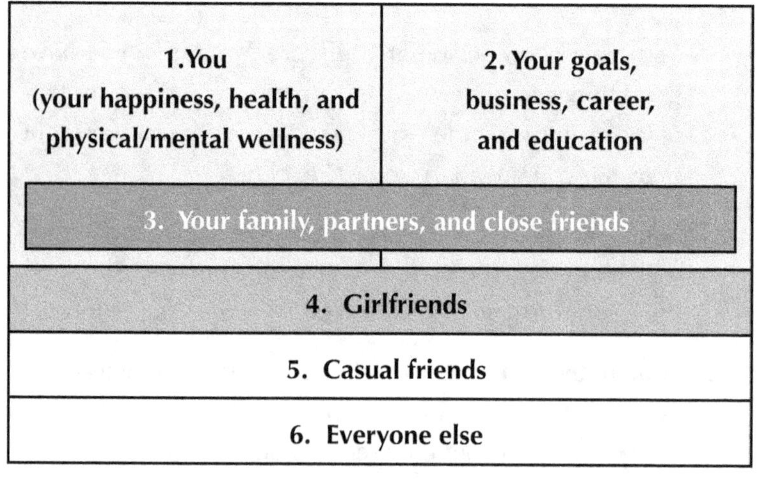

1.You
(your happiness, health, and physical/mental wellness)
2. Your goals, business, career, and education
3. Your family, partners, and close friends
4. Girlfriends
5. Casual friends
6. Everyone else

Think of this as running an organization. You are the boss or CEO at the top, the vital one making it all happen and taking care of everyone and everything. In this analogy, you are currently recruiting applicants for a Level 4 position. You don't bring in new people higher than Level 4. They need to earn higher levels. Level 4 people are treated wonderfully and she will like being at this level.

It is good to be at Level 4, but great to be promoted to and enjoy the added perks of Level 3 (i.e., wife or partner). She needs to be someone you want at Level 3, and her conduct and behavior need to align with what you need of people at Level 3. To be clear, it is possible to be fired from or demoted within the organization due to conduct.

Does this sound selfish? It isn't. It is selfless. This arrangement isn't for your benefit. You are doing all that work to improve and build out Levels 1 and 2 every day not for yourself, but to be as valuable of an asset for people at Level 3—those closest to you—as you can be. You work hard to support them and so that they can thrive. You do it all for her, your family, your children, and any others who you care the most about in this world. Women will like it when they see how you operate, and why you do as you do—for others. This philosophy will be powerfully cool and attractive to her. It's allure to her will be almost magical. If she doesn't feel that way, another lady who will appreciate and admire your approach will be along shortly.

## The Ten Rules

You feel confident, know exactly what you are looking for, and are ready to roll! Time to meet some people, right? Let's do that, but in a manner governed by a few essential rules to help improve your chances of success.

Below are Ten Rules you should always adhere to—not just when meeting new ladies, but all the time:

1. Be confident.
2. Have a plan. Always have something to say.
3. She needs to feel safe, comfortable, and unthreatened at all times.
4. Every interaction must be a positive experience for her throughout.
5. Don't be creepy.
6. Don't harass.
7. Never at your workplace or place of business.
8. Pre-screen and assess the situation and environment.
9. Smile and make eye contact.
10. Listen to her. Watch her body language.

What do these Ten Rules mean? Let's elaborate on each of them.

### RULE 1: *Be confident.*

You know that, if things work out, she is better off with you. It will improve her life. You know this is true, but she doesn't—yet.

What are your sources of confidence? As we discussed earlier, it isn't an act. Natural confidence flowing from how you live, and who you are, is so crucial to our process it bears repeating:

1. You are a good person at your core. You know you have good things to offer. You have a plan, are serious, and aren't wasting her time.
2. You know that even her most protective family and friends will like you. Her parents will welcome you. She, and they, can trust you.
3. You are the type of person she can build a life with, and raise a family, if that is what you both want. You are the type of man your children will be proud of.
4. You are prepared, and you have good intentions, high integrity, and unrivaled depth of character. These things, plus the way you conduct yourself in all matters every day, make you highly desirable.

Some studies say people form their first impressions of others within the first four to seven seconds of meeting. That short time might sound impossible to control or influence in any meaningful way, but if your confidence is authentic and flows from the sources we discussed, that good initial impression will happen naturally.

You will automatically project confidence because you know you are coming from a good place, and you will find that people are more drawn to you the more you live up to these standards. You know you will make a good boyfriend, husband, or father as surely as you know the sun will rise tomorrow.

Maybe think about this way: Some lady's life will soon improve in a high-quality way, and it just might be the life of the next lady you decide to meet.

**RULE 2: *Have a plan. Always have something to say.***

Be prepared, be calm, and have a plan. You've already carefully thought through and created your compatibility assessment, right? You know you are a good person, but you want to learn more about her. There is something about her that you feel might be interesting. Now is the time to break the ice.

Don't let a good opportunity pass you by. You might regret it for the rest of your life.

**TIP:** A secret to always having something to say, and working up the courage to say it . . .

When you see someone you want to meet, first imagine her as being a cherished, long-time friend. Picture her as someone with whom you are entirely comfortable discussing anything. How nervous would you be making small talk with someone like that, or just saying hi and asking how she is doing, and caring about her answer? You would be yourself—confident, happy to see her, and looking forward to the interaction. You'd be sporting a natural, genuine smile. Try it.

As the dozens of interactions you will have in the first few days turn into hundreds in the coming weeks to thousands over the years, all of this will become second nature to you. And it will be fun for both of you!

### SAFETY TIP

Please carefully consider what contact information you are willing to share with her this early. For your personal security, maybe share nothing beyond a mobile phone number. What number should you give her? Do not give out your work or business number unless you are certain she can be trusted. Another option is to use the video call feature of a social media app like Instagram, Facebook Messenger, or many others. They don't require giving out your phone number.

Be careful about giving out too much information, for your own privacy and safety, should something go wrong. Maybe just use your first name and mobile number (not a home number). Consider using a second, disposable, pay-as-you-go mobile phone, but be aware using one might make her suspicious. Consider carrying a few contact cards. This isn't a modern approach, but if it fits your style, then use it. Business cards you print at home are fine.

**RULE 3:** ***She needs to feel safe, comfortable, and unthreatened at all times.***

Never lose sight of the fact that she needs to always feel safe with you, from the initial approach onward. You want to approach her confidently, but in a fun way. You goal is to get her to WANT to lower her defenses, not to force your way past them or trick her in some way. You want her to trust you from the very start.

You are the real deal. You are trustworthy, serious, and interested in her for good reasons. Let that show.

**RULE 4:** ***Every interaction must be a positive experience for her throughout.***

No matter what happens, the lady must *always* feel good about her interaction with you – never regretting that she spent time meeting and speaking with you. Always end the conversation (or date, or relationship) in a positive way, even if she doesn't do the same, and even if she treats you poorly.

**RULE 5:** ***Don't act creepy.***

Basically, don't do anything to scare her on approach, or while you are interacting. Don't stare at her prior to approach. Don't scare her by sneaking up from behind her. Don't block her ability to leave or move around. In conversation, be mindful of the impact of what you are saying, and avoid complimenting her too much, making sexual references, or discussing her body or appearance too much. For example, too many men spend too much time gushing about how gorgeous a woman is, and that often doesn't have the impact he thinks it does.

**RULE 6: *Don't harass.***

Take "no" for an answer. Once she has given you a firm "no," or her body language says "no" or "go away," then respect that. Smile, say goodbye nicely and wish her a good day, per Rule 4.

**RULE 7: *Never at your workplace or place of business.***

I strongly recommend NOT flirting or dating at your place of business or work. This can cost you your job, customers, or clients if things go badly. Since pretty much the rest of the world is fair game, you can live with excluding the place where you earn your living. You don't need trouble at work or in the office.

There is a common misapprehension out there that flirting takes place only in certain places like parties, bars, or nightclubs. The best way to think about this is to consider your flirting zone, with a few reasonable exceptions (e.g., your workplace, funerals, crime scenes and disaster areas), nearly *everywhere* else on the planet. That includes most places you regularly go every day: the grocery store, the gym, the local mall, out for a walk on the street, the gas station, or the store where you buy socks.

Mingling, approaches, introductions, and socializing are expected at some places, but less so in others. A lady at a party or a bar might be more mentally prepared for your approach than one at a store, the mall, or out in public somewhere. Sometimes fast-paced, busy cities are more difficult places to successfully pull off approaches compared to slower-paced areas. A woman's sense of safety and comfort might be different in a crowded city scene or a dark parking lot. There also might be cultural differences or norms in a country or region that make this more difficult, or easier—it just depends.

No matter what, you should still confidently try, while staying within the bounds of acceptable behavior. Just remember, a reasonable amount of confidence—even audacity—is fine. Vital, even.

### RULE 8: *Pre-screen and assess the situation and environment.*

You will want to avoid unnecessary trouble on approach. Check her for engagement or wedding rings (left hand, ring finger). Don't approach others' wives and girlfriends. Approach no one who is underage. Also, avoid ladies in groups of protective guys. There is no need for a potential confrontation. There are far too many eligible, single women out there.

Be keenly alert to your surroundings and the overall situation. Be observant. Also, quickly and unobtrusively look her over her for signs of health, hygiene, and drug or alcohol abuse.

### RULE 9. *Smile and make eye contact.*

Smile. A genuine, "whole face" smile is best. Let your eyes naturally squint a little. Use a mirror to see the difference between your "mouth-only smile" and your "whole face smile." How do you naturally smile when you see a cute baby, puppy, or kitten, or a beloved close friend or family member? Go with the smile that shows the real you, and the one you are comfortable with.

Have a twinkle or sparkle in your eyes, not a leering gaze. This helps her feel and see that you have good intentions. She will sense your positive energy.

Make eye contact, but do not stare. Make her see you as fun and playful—someone she wants to spend time with.

### RULE 10: *Listen to her. Watch her body language.*

Be respectful and interested in her as a person. Carefully listen to what she says. Be observant of her body language cues. Is her body language showing fear? A level of comfort? Playfulness? Openness? Interest, or a lack of it?

Mind your body language as well. What is it saying about you? What is it telling her? Some studies tell us that between 80 and 90% of communication is body language and tonality. The remaining 10–20% is your actual words or what you say. Use a more "open" type of body language. For example, don't cross your arms. Face her with your feet pointed toward her. If you tend to talk with your hands, use open, more expansive gestures. Maintain a good and relaxed posture.

Speak with a confident tone, deepen your voice, and speak slowly. Finally, have fun!

> "The best way to predict your future is to create it."
> —Abraham Lincoln

## REALITY CHECK: SURVEY RESULTS

To make sure I am giving you the best possible advice, I surveyed a large number of ladies who could arguably be considered among the very best in the world. I reached out to famous and accomplished ladies from a variety of fields and walks of life, including actresses from movies and television, Olympic gold medal-winning athletes, and major national and international beauty contest winners. I did this because I thought obtaining a variety of perspectives from women who many might consider models of excellence, or maybe unattainable, might be helpful. I am grateful that so many of them took the time to thoughtfully respond.

Here are some of the most common themes across the responses and feedback I received:

> **Having a plan is good.** There was strong support for the idea of a man being thoughtful and intentional about what's going to get a woman's attention.
>
> **Be honest.** One strongly recurring theme was that being honest helps build trust and helps her feel safe with you. The ladies surveyed pointed out it was important for people to be willing to be honest about who they are even from the very first conversation. They felt that, if you can be honest about yourself, then the woman can feel safe being honest about herself.
>
> **Be genuine. Be yourself.** This came up in several forms. Basically, those surveyed said women aren't looking for a knight in shining armor or the best pick-up line. They're just looking for someone who is

genuine. Sentiment toward classic pick-up lines was negative across the board. They felt if you stay true to yourself, you will come across as much more confident.

**Get to know her.** Another strong theme throughout the responses was that the guys who stand out are the ones who are truly interested in getting to know the lady. They suggest not just talking about yourself too much. The consensus was that it is best when the conversation is a back-and-forth where the two people get to know each other like real adults. These ladies advised you to be open, bold, strong, and honest.

**Relax. Be cool and have fun.** This theme ties the rest together. Here, they suggest that what works better in their dating experience have been the guys who were the most relaxed and casual, who said something funny or made a kind of light compliment. They also suggest having a smile on your face. Basically, they recommended always being yourself, as well as being friendly and genuine.

Not one woman surveyed said they like being showered with praise. They don't want anyone to go on about how beautiful they are, or to otherwise put them on some sort of pedestal. A lot of men make this mistake on approach or early on in conversations.

To close this section, all the survey responses were condensed into this word cloud to give you a visual sense of the consensus from the survey. This is distilled wisdom from a group of some of the best women on the planet. It is advice straight from accomplished, famous, award-winning, and world-stage gold-medalist ladies at the top of their respective fields. If you prefer to picture it coming from a single composite source, it is advice straight to you from the most brilliant, deep, creative, and beautiful superwoman imaginable.

Relationship Comfortable
Confident Beautiful
Real Authentic Impressed True
Amaze Welcoming Truth Surprise
Priorities Date Serious Respond Value
Genuine Enjoy Human Intelligent
Romantic Happy
Radiates Funny Gentleman Smart
Sexy Heart Nice Normal
Intentional Warm Honest Friendly
Exchange
Soul Optimism Integrity Kind Charm
Fun Thoughts Happiness Respect Feelings
Confidence Thoughtful
Beauty Sweet Casual Wisdom Interest Relaxed
Melted Open Attracted Positive
Together
Like Love Sincerity Partner
Energy Old-school
Polite Patience Compliment

EDUCATION
CAREER
GIVING
BACK
YOU
INTIMACY
RELATIONSHIPS
STARTING A FAMILY
BUSINESS
GOALS

# PART 1

# Part 2.
# MEETING IN-PERSON

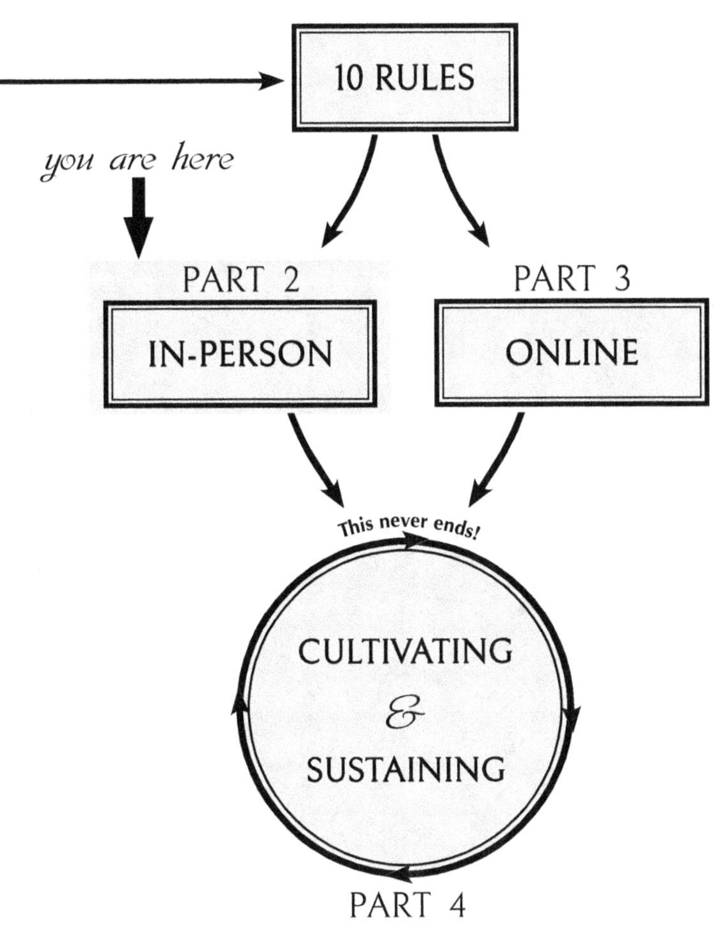

> "Love, like Fortune, favors the bold"
>
> —Ovid line I.608 of Ars Amatoria

Here we lay out a comprehensive process and mindset for meeting great ladies in person that works with plenty of examples that can be used right away.

A lady has caught your eye in public, at a social gathering, or in some other real-world setting. You want to meet her. What are you going to do? Is there something that stops you? Is it lack of confidence, not feeling comfortable about what to say at first, not knowing how she might react to your approach, or not feeling comfortable carrying on a meaningful and constructive conversation with her? No matter what your situation is, I have you covered.

What works? Following the basic steps below will help, as will always remaining in accordance with our Ten Rules. You should also be prepared, have good intentions and a positive attitude, and execute these steps in a fun and relaxed way.

As a reminder, here are our Ten Rules from Part 1. Always adhere to these rules no matter where you are in the process: today, a month into it, or years later.

1. Be confident.
2. Have a plan. Always have something to say.
3. She needs to feel safe, comfortable, and unthreatened at all times.
4. Every interaction must be a positive experience for her throughout.
5. Don't be creepy.
6. Don't harass.
7. Never at your workplace or place of business.
8. Pre-screen and assess the situation and environment.
9. Smile and make eye contact.
10. Listen to her. Watch her body language.

Here are the basic steps for meeting someone in person:

**STEP 1.** ***You keep getting better every day through your continuous improvement.***
***You are constantly executing Step 1.***

We covered this in Part 1. This is core to our whole process and is the source of the natural confidence and energy you need to project.

**STEP 2.** ***You notice someone interesting.***

Who you find interesting and attractive is entirely up to you. I am giving you the tools to meet and connect with whomever that is. I want to be crystal clear that no woman is out of your league, no matter how beautiful, wealthy, or famous she is—not one. You can meet someone just about anywhere— the grocery store, the gym, or most other places you find yourself in your daily life. Don't limit yourself to just bars, parties, and nightclubs. Remember to avoid work or the office per Rule 7.

**STEP 3.** ***You pre-screen and pre-assess before making any approach.***

This step aligns with Rule 8 from our Ten Rules.

You will want to avoid unnecessary trouble on the approach. Check her for engagement or wedding rings (left hand, ring finger). Don't approach others' wives and girlfriends. Approach no one who is underage. Avoid ladies in groups of protective guys. Also, quickly and unobtrusively look her over her for signs of health, hygiene, and drug or alcohol abuse.

**STEP 4.** ***Make contact. What is she thinking when you do?***

Her safety is at the top of her mind: Who is this person? Is he a threat in any way? What does he want? Is this casual, friendly, someone I know saying "Hi," do I have a spider crawling in my hair, or is he hitting on me?

She is forming her first impression of you. Many studies have shown that you have only four to seven seconds to make that first impression.

Four to seven seconds isn't much time. How the heck are you supposed to present yourself in a positive light so quickly? You do that by projecting your natural confidence and positive energy, as well as your genuine smile, good intentions toward her, relaxed and non-threatening posture, preparation, and greeting.

She might need a moment to process what just happened. Some women are confident and reply or react quickly. Others hesitate. It just depends on each individual lady. There isn't a right or wrong to it.

Keep reading for more on how to start and sustain the conversation with her.

**STEP 5. *More screening during the conversation.***

Find out about her bit-by-bit, in a friendly, natural, and human exchange. Don't come off like you are interrogating her against your compatibility assessment criteria, it might be too early to touch on much of that. At this point you want to know if she is available and interested. This is crucial. Is she fun and interesting? Are you feeling any chemistry? What percentage of your assessment criteria from Part 1 do you think she might meet as you learn about her later?

**STEP 6. *If all goes well, transition to a quick date or get her contact information. If not, revert to Step 1.***

Be bold yet impeccably respectful. Also, consider your privacy and personal safety when giving out contact information, but at the same time act in a way that shows you are genuinely interested in her, open, and trustworthy.

**STEP 7. (covered in Part 4) *Over one or more dates, you explore her match potential based on your compatibility assessment criteria from Part 1. If she is, then consider progressing to a relationship or girlfriend status over time. If not, revert to Step 1.***

Note there is no shortcut provision above that says anything like if she is extraordinarily pretty or hot, or if you are lonely, then quickly move in together. The various screening and assessment steps in our process are intentional, necessary, and mandatory.

The steps above sound reasonable enough, right? But how exactly do you accomplish this? There's no magic solution here. There is nothing you can say or do that will guarantee every woman says "yes." There are lots of ways to succeed and lots of ways to fail at in-person approaches. Possibilities for failed approaches are she might be unavailable, too busy to talk, or is otherwise not interested in this exchange for various reasons. That is okay because plenty of women will be interested and open to you over time. Be patient. Our process works.

***Meeting Women in Groups***

You may be in a social situation and find yourself attracted to someone who is in a group of people. Your first problem is that you don't know her situation. Your second problem, specific to groups, is you don't know who all those guys and girls in the group are. One could be her dad, boyfriend, husband, or a protective friend.

The right approach, no matter what, is to be respectful to everyone in the group. Don't fake it—you must feel and project real and heartfelt respect. Don't approach the lady you are interested in directly since you don't know her situation yet. The group might become concerned about your intentions, and you might get run off quickly and forcefully by a husband, boyfriend, dad, brother, or protective friend.

However, if you are friendly and respectful to everyone, the reception you receive is more likely to be favorable. If you go in aggressively like a shark or wolf, directly at her, her social circle may decide they need to close ranks around her and expel you. It is better to approach the group with genuine respect and converse with everyone in a natural and friendly way as you work toward figuring out if she is available and someone you might be interested in.

> You need to get to a point where being comfortable meeting women is second nature to you and something you look forward to doing. You also need to get to a point where you don't fear rejection, and rejection doesn't affect you at all. This takes practice—there is no other way. There is nothing wrong with taking a chance and being told "no."

## Getting Started

Since I don't know everyone's skill level, I want to start with the basics. Then we will build from there.

Before we start, I need to describe the format of these conversations and what's in them:

| IN-PERSON or ONLINE | CONVERSATION <number>. |
|---|---|
| **Part 2 lists "In-person" here, and Part 3 lists "Online".** | **I numbered these to make it easy to refer to them (e.g. IN-PERSON \| CONVERSATION 27 or ONLINE \| CONVERSATION 14). In-person is Part 2 of the book, and Online is Part 3.** |

**SITUATION:** You will see these conversation boxes throughout Parts 2 and 3.
1) There might be a short explanation in this section of the circumstances or scene at the top like this.
2) Here we'll have some example dialog.

**You:** Crisply deliver a clever, respectful, and thoughtful opening line.

**Her:** She is wow'ed, flattered, and interested

**You:** Bring more playful and fun energy as you work toward learning a bit about her.

**Her:** She loves it as conversation progresses… and so on …

### NOTES AND OBSERVATIONS

3) Here is where my commentary and notes to you will be.

I understand a lot of you will be nervous at least the first few times you try these various approaches. Being nervous is completely natural. Learn to harness that extra energy to your advantage and bring it to your interaction with her. To help calm those nerves, remember:

1. You are a great guy with good intentions. You are someone who is improving himself every day. If she is in the market, you are likely exactly what she is looking for. She is just walking around right now not knowing that fact, or that you exist. You are about to correct that.

2. You know what you want. You have thoughtfully created your compatibility assessment criteria in Part 1. You are serious about meeting and connecting with a great woman. She likely isn't accustomed to meeting a man like you. But she wants to. Who wouldn't?

3. You strictly adhere to our Ten Rules.

4. As I suggested elsewhere, in your own mind, think of her as a close personal friend who you have known for years. Treat her like that from the very start. What tone of voice do you use with such a person? You'd naturally smile with them. You'd have no problems with nervousness, right? Use this mental trick on yourself – you will like it, and she will feel your positive energy and appreciate your tone and your relaxed manner.

5. As for having something to say, we have many opener ideas here for you. We also list some general use conversation extenders later below, with more to come in Part 4 (where you prepare for full dates and building toward a

possible relationship). You have the items in your compatibility assessment criteria to draw on later, as the conversation progresses and you feel it is time to learn more about her. You also can, without bragging, mention some of your recent wins or what you are working on from your daily continuous improvement process.

6. You have the benefit of the philosophy and distilled wisdom in this book backing you.

Next, because we are starting from the very beginning, I want to assign you an exercise.

**EXERCISE 1**

Over the next few weeks, as you progress through the material in this book or until you feel perfectly comfortable doing this, I want you to smile at and make eye contact with 100 women. There is no need to say anything if you don't want to. Or you can just smile, say "Hello," and continue on your way. Many women will reply and some won't, and either outcome is fine. The purpose of this exercise is to get you comfortable with speaking up, seeing how everyday women react to your unexpected greeting, and seeing that nothing bad will come from doing so.

When you are completely at ease with Exercise 1, consider the conversation example below as a next step in your progression:

## IN-PERSON | CONVERSATION 1

**SITUATION:** You see an interesting lady anywhere in your daily life. She, you, and the situation are all okay per our Ten Rules.

**You:** Hi! How are you?

**Her:** *<could be Hello, could be nothing, could be a short or very long reply>*

### NOTES AND OBSERVATIONS

As simple as this example looks on the surface, there's magic in it when delivered effectively. The key is here is to say "Hi" with a smile, plus what tonality and energy you put into the "How are you?". Try it yourself in the mirror. First, say it flatly, in a monotone way like you are just being polite to someone you don't like, and you really hope the other person doesn't answer. Next, say it with a genuine smile on your face, with more energy, like you are happy to see a cherished friend you want to spend time with, and you honestly want to know how they are doing. In that second case, you might without thinking give the "Hi" a little extra energy, and you might raise the volume a little as you work through the "How are you?", smiling the whole time. Which form do you think lands better on another person's ears, getting a positive reaction? Her response can be anything from nothing at all the way to a full explanation of how she is doing at that moment. Some ladies are friendly, love to talk, and will immediately and completely open up to a guy who she immediately feels she can trust, who sounds fun, and who is bold and self-confident enough to approach her out of the blue. You'll see.

## EXERCISE 2

Switch to "Hello there! How Are you?" from Conversation 1 above for this exercise. But feel free to do that as a "drive-by flirt," meaning you can say that in passing and not wait for a response. I don't mean blurt it out and then sprint away. This phrasing is a perfectly acceptable and friendly greeting to say to strangers in passing as you go about your normal day. There is normally no need to stop and respond back should she say anything unless you feel comfortable doing so. Do this with 100 women, or until it starts feeling second nature to you. Repeat this process until it comes as naturally to you as breathing, and you can clearly visualize taking the next step - continuing the conversation with the ladies who reply and seem open to talking more.

## IN-PERSON | CONVERSATION 2

**SITUATION:** You see an interesting lady anywhere in your daily life. She, you, and the situation are all okay per our Ten Rules.

**You:** Hi Pretty! How are you?

**Her:** *<could be Hello, could be nothing, could be a long reply>*

### NOTES AND OBSERVATIONS

"Hi Pretty! How are you?" might be the greatest opener of all time. It has everything you need in the fewest possible words. You have the compliment upfront. Then you immediately defuse that jarring statement by asking her something she can use to start the conversation with you, just like in Conversation 1 above. It respectfully tells her that you are attracted to her but doesn't stop to awkwardly dwell on that point being made so early. Again, don't say this in a flat, monotone voice. Don't deliver it in a way that might feel creepy (refer to Part 1) to her. Have a warm and friendly smile on your face as you deliver the line. You'll see me use other forms of this in examples below, but in those cases, it might be "Hi Pretty! <ask legitimate question/ask for advice/jokingly give her a fun task to do>". For in-person openers, this one—in all its forms—is pure gold.

Let's look at a couple more examples where we don't try to close on the spot, meaning asking for her contact information or a date. We are working up to perform Exercise 3, which is coming up soon.

## IN-PERSON | CONVERSATION 3

**SITUATION:** You are shopping for very large coffee cups for yourself, and only finding normal sizes. A pretty woman walks up the aisle you are in.

**You:** <*without looking at her, but smiling*> Hi Pretty! How are you?

**Her:** <*she laughs*> good?

**You:** Hey, if you see any super large coffee mugs, microwave safe, give me some sort of a signal. CawCaw like a bird, or something like that.

**Her:** Got it. Cawcaw. <*laughs as she practices*>

**You:** You're the best! <*laughs*><*you continue looking*>

**Her:** <*she pauses to think*> Would a soup mug work?

<She's in. Continue the conversation. Thank her for her help when you two are done, if you don't instead want to try to close with her.>

## NOTES AND OBSERVATIONS

Remember what I suggested about treating women that you would like to meet like a long-time and dear friend? Try this. You will see it repeatedly work in your daily practice. Many people are nice and quick to offer help. Now, in this case, she knows from your "Hi Pretty" that you are likely flirting with her, but you went straight into drafting her into helping you with what you were already doing. She might not be shocked by someone flirting with her; guys do that with pretty women all the time. But what she isn't accustomed to is a stranger who just flirted with her giving her a task to do like you are already close friends or a couple. We will have longer and more complete examples like this later. For now, I wanted to show how you can transition from a playful, flirty greeting to a natural human conversation in seconds. There is no need for complex gimmicks. There is no need for pickup lines. Within seconds, you can make a good impression with her on a subconscious level and go from the shock and awe of a bold and flirtatious comment to a real conversation. And, as a bonus, you might find those king-sized coffee mugs you went there for in the first place.

## IN-PERSON | CONVERSATION 4

**SITUATION:** It's Friday night and you are at a grocery store. You want to pay for your groceries. You see a pretty cashier and get in her line.

**Her:** Hi! Did you find everything?

**You:** Hi Pretty! How are you? Yes, I've got everything.

**Her:** <*surprised*> thank you!

**You:** Why do they have you here working so late? Aren't you supposed to be out living the exciting lifestyle of beautiful people?

**Her:** Me? What exciting lifestyle? When I go home, I'm going to sleep. Between classes and work, I don't have a lot of free time.

*<Yes, she left an opening in her response that you could respond to, and we do normally look for those to continue the conversation and get a sense if she is available. She sounds like a single person with a lackluster social life. You could be thinking about asking for her number at this point, but please read the commentary below first.>*

## NOTES AND OBSERVATIONS

If you need practice, practice with the best. Use every opportunity. In this mundane example, you have an example where you get into lines with the prettiest cashiers in stores to practice. This isn't a bad or creepy thing to do because you have your Ten Rules, and you are always perfectly respectful of everyone. Be playful. (I have polled a lot of guys over the years, and the majority get in the line with the prettiest cashier just for fun, even if the line is longer. There's no shame in that!) But remember the ladies are working and aren't there to be hit on, or worse still, harassed. However, most ladies don't mind a light compliment to brighten up their day as long as you take care not to embarrass them. You might see these same ladies in your community when they are off work, and they are likely to remember you in a positive way from the fun way you treat them at work. Don't be surprised if they take the chance to flirt back when they see you outside of work.

My last item is more of a suggestion: You might want to make sure that you meet some minimum standard for grooming and how you are dressed whenever you are in public. I am not saying you need to always be camera-ready. Still, if you are going to be out there flirting 24/7 with your newfound knowledge and confidence, you might want to hold yourself to dressing and grooming accordingly before leaving home. I am a guy like you. I understand completely. I am fine with walking around as a grass-stained, mud-splattered mess in tattered clothes, but that isn't presenting yourself to your best advantage if you subscribe to our philosophy that your flirting zone is the entire world. You never know when you will meet someone great.

## IN-PERSON | CONVERSATION 5

**SITUATION:** A lovely and fit woman is standing by herself outside of the gym. You see no potential Ten Rule-related problems, and walk over to her so that she can see you coming.

**You:** *<smiling>* Hi Pretty! You look like you are a model for this place. Camera-ready. And you look like you are ready for gold at the Olympics.

**Her:** *<laughs>* Funny you should say that. I ran track in high school and college.

**You:** Ahhhh.

**Her:** *<she goes into a longer story about her athletic background>*

**You:** *<listen without interrupting, since you are just learning about someone new>*
*<ask for her name when there is a break, and introduce yourself>*

**You:** Pleased to meet you!
*<continue the conversation using something she said that you found interesting from the personal story she shared with you>*

## NOTES AND OBSERVATIONS

This is a very typical example. You see a lady you are interested in meeting, and you attempt to do so in a manner aligned with the Ten Rules and following our general approach. Your opening here is unique and flattering. It is a variation on the "Hi Pretty" theme. It doubles the compliments related to her appearance, but immediately lets her off the hook with the "ready for gold at the Olympics" comment. You quickly learn that fitness is a passion of hers. You actively listen to what she says without interruption, your body language and actions show interest, and you laugh when she attempts humor whether you find it funny or not. Here again, you listen to what she is saying and how she says it, looking for possible hooks to continue the conversation, learn more about her, and work toward a possible close later (i.e. ask for a quick date now, or get her contact information).

## EXERCISE 3

Switch to mixing in some form of "Hi Pretty! How are you?" when you find a particular lady attractive and there is no violation of our Ten Rules. There is "Hi Pretty! How are you?," "Hi Pretty! <Ask a legitimate question>," "Hi Pretty! <Ask for advice>," and "Hi Pretty! <Give her a fun task to do>" to use. You'll like the results from "Hi Pretty..." in real life.

As you work through Exercise 3 in the real world, you will quickly find out how well our process works, and you will need to be able to handle several different types of situations that will arise. As for the conversations themselves, those can go millions of ways, and obviously, we cannot cover every permutation. But we will cover our general principles on successfully navigating in-person approaches. We do that in the next, more complicated series of conversation examples that follow. Please pay attention to what's in the "Notes and Observations" section of each.

Before we get into that, I want to define what I mean by "conversation extender" clearly. You'll see that while executing an opener is easy, still you need to be able to initiate, lead, and hold up your end of the conversation with her. Good sources of conversation topics for this early stage of meeting someone include: listen to what she says and ask about whatever parts interest you, ask her for her advice or opinion on something relevant to where you are or what you are doing, ask her about herself and her interests, and maybe draw on some of the less heavy items from your compatibility assessment criteria from Part 1 (e.g., don't ask if she wants to get married and have a baby so early). You can also talk about recent wins from your ongoing push toward your goals and daily self-improvement, but stop short of bragging.

If the conversation stalls or you are having trouble getting started using the ideas above, consider some form of these general-purpose conversation extenders:

Where are you from?

Are you local, from around here?

What's new?

What do you do?

How are you doing?

What's going on?

What are you up to today?

Any plans for this weekend?

What do you do in your free time?

What do you think about... ?

## Putting it all Together

### IN-PERSON | CONVERSATION 6

**SITUATION:** You are out in public and see a woman of extraordinary beauty. Per our process, the Ten Rules always apply even when you are staggered by her appearance.

**You:** Excuse me. I mean this in the nicest possible way. Of all the pretty ladies I have seen here today, you are head and shoulders far more pretty. It's not even close.

**Her:** *<is slightly stunned>* Oh my god, thank you!

**You:** Whatever it is you are doing, keep doing it.

**Her:** Good to know!

**You:** *<It is time to transition off of her appearance to something else>* Hey, I believe you have expertise that I don't. What around here serves healthy food that tastes good, and that I will like?

**Her:** *<laughs>* The good taste part of that isn't easy, but I'd suggest _______, which is nearby.

**You:** Does that have seating, or is it carryout?

**Her:** Yeah, they have tables.

**You:** Have you eaten? Come with me. My travel guide. My treat.

**Her:** Ummmm. Sure. Okay.

*<Off you two go. Now you start having a normal human conversation with her, leaving the heavy compliments, shocking openers, and other gimmicks behind. While still being fun and playful, you are now slowly trying to see if you feel there might be any chemistry between you. By chemistry, I mean, at the highest level, do you get a sense you two might share some of the same values and want the same things. Chemistry can be a sign there might be compatibility. To answer the larger question of compatibility, our process calls for creating the compatibility assessments back in Part 1.>*

## NOTES AND OBSERVATIONS

The Ten Rules are non-negotiable, even when you are blown away by her appearance. Focus, and don't break discipline! Your opening here is about as far as you should normally go with dwelling on her appearance. You made your point emphatically and in a way she will fondly remember for a long time. A mistake I see a lot of guys making is that they rave about the lady's appearance and how hot she is. That is very awkward and uncomfortable for her to hear and deal with. It makes the guy sound like he is purely interested in sex. It is OK to pay a compliment and tell her how pretty she is, but you need to move on to something else very quickly to be as successful as possible. Again, I suggest treating her like an existing friend. I like the assertiveness of "Come with me. My treat." Here you asked her to join you in something that you wanted to do anyway, and who doesn't want the prettiest woman in a 5-mile radius as your lunch partner. If nothing else, the food will taste better. Win-win.

## IN-PERSON | CONVERSATION 7

**SITUATION:** It's a party or social gathering of some sort, both you and her are guests but you don't know her. She is by herself.

**You:** Walk up to her, making sure she knows you are there so you won't startle her. Reach out to shake her hand saying "Hi! I don't think we've met before, I'm *<first name>*.

**Her:** Hi! I'm Ashley.

**You:** Nice to meet you Ashley! This place is great!

**Her:** It's amazing!

**You:** How do you know the host? *<or whatever conversation extender feels natural at this point>*

## NOTES AND OBSERVATIONS

Most of the examples I provide here are in a normal public setting. However, in some situations like a party, mingling is expected between people who don't know each other. That makes the approach easier. There are a couple points I want to make in this example. The first is the addition of "I don't think we've met before" to your greeting. Adding that makes it sound like you are someone she should know and should want to know. That also adds energy to the conversation right out of the gate. Most people don't introduce themselves in a way that implies that the two of you should have already met. My second point is around the use of her name. You asked for her name, which is good and polite. But now, you need to use her name in conversation to help connect. Repeating her name also helps you remember it; you don't want to embarrass yourself and possibly insult her by forgetting what she shared.

## IN-PERSON | CONVERSATION 8

**SITUATION:** It's a party or social gathering of some sort, both you and her are guests but you don't know her.

**You:** You make eye contact, with a polite but playful smile, and maybe a little wave. You say nothing unless she reacts.

**Her:** Hi?

**You:** I noticed you across the room, and had to introduce myself. I'm *<first name>*.

**Her:** I'm Bethany.

**You:** Bethany, you look stunning tonight. Your dress is such an interesting color. Where did you find that, it looks high end designer quality?

**Her:** *<she tells you the story>*

<ice is now broken, continue the conversation>

## NOTES AND OBSERVATIONS

A couple points here:

1) Who said you had to make first contact verbally? Here you make light eye contact from a distance. Note that I didn't stay stare her down until she looks back. Just use a relaxed glance here and there to see if you can catch her eye. If you can, smile and give her a little wave. You might get ignored, an eye roll, or a friendly reply. If you get rejected or ignored, do nothing and brush it off. (Rejection happens and is okay, you are going to get a point later where rejection doesn't affect you at all).

2) Saying "You look stunning tonight" is bold, yet correct. But it is a heavy compliment that you need to not let awkwardly hang in the air. She might be uncomfortable with that, since she does not know your intentions yet. So, don't wait for her to reply, move to your other point to move the conversation along. She knows you find her attractive from what you said before, now move on to getting to know her a bit.

## IN-PERSON | CONVERSATION 9

**SITUATION:** Your both are leaving the same building. It's raining heavily, and you have a long walk to your car. She is waiting at the door for the rain to subside before she leaves.

**You:** Those are some mighty big raindrops.
You know what, it would be awesome if you would go get my car, and bring it here—close to the door. Then I will drive you to your car.

**Her:** *<laughs>* I'll get wet!

**You:** You look like a fast runner.

**Her:** *<laughs>* I don't think so.

**You:** I guess I'll wait. I'm *<first name>*. I don't think we've met...

**Her:** I'm Becky. Hi!

**You:** Nice to meet you!
*<You transition to something else and continue the conversation>*
It looks like the rain is about to let us leave. Hey, can I have you number?

**Her:** Sure.

## NOTES AND OBSERVATIONS

Humorously asking her to do something outrageous yet harmless is good opening material. Be careful; she could take you up on the offer and steal your car, so don't go through with it if she calls your bluff. No lady in my experience has ever said yes to this one. You got her attention with your unique opening and calm, flawless delivery. Getting her name was good; just remember to use it here and there as the conversation progresses. Nature eventually gave you both a reason to leave, so you didn't have to make up an excuse and get drenched. Whenever you needed to go was the perfect time to ask for her contact information. Perfection!

## IN-PERSON | CONVERSATION 10

**SITUATION:** You are in a store staring at a display with boxes of chocolate, debating whether you should indulge. A lady nearby notices you.

**Her:** *<makes eye contact with you>* I used to live near where those are made.

**You:** ahhh. Nice!

**Her:** We could smell the confections baking in our house . . . *<She continues her story>*

**You:** *<You're trying to listen, but quickly notice that she has incredibly pretty blue eyes, and are now having trouble paying attention>*
*<You decide to grab a box for yourself>*
Hey, let me pick up one of these for you.

**Her:** Oh, no. No thanks! That was so sweet of you!

**You:** I need to run to an appointment. Can I your number?

**Her:** Sure.

## NOTES AND OBSERVATIONS

You don't have to make the first move every time. Sometimes the lady approaches you. What draws them to do so? It is your confidence, the energy you project, your look, your clothes, your grooming, and how you carry yourself. Being handsome adds a few points, but it is all the other factors that mean more. For example, one of the testers for this book is a handsome guy in his early 20s. He is also calm, poised, and well-spoken. He gets approached by women roughly 3 times per day on average at his public-facing job. In some cases, young women send their mother to where he works to give him their phone number.

Sometimes I see older female relatives will ask a man if he is married on behalf of their daughter's or nieces when they see a man who clearly has himself together and carries himself well.

Regarding this conversation, looking at her eyes was OK while she was talking. Staring at her breasts or mouth wouldn't have been OK. Be careful where your eyes go when you are talking to a woman. She can see what you are doing. You didn't hear everything she said in this case, but she doesn't know you lost focus. You did your best, but those eyes were so unfair.

One final point, depending on the circumstances, sometimes you can be firm about getting her phone number or contact information. I mean you can try nicely, but firmly, telling her to give you her number instead of asking "can I have" or "please may I." Your tone of voice needs to be appropriate for that. I would say asking for contact information should be your go-to move, but I wanted to show you this other option.

## IN-PERSON | CONVERSATION 11

**SITUATION:** You want to check out a popular bar you've heard about. You go inside and look around. You see a lady wearing what looks like office clothes, sitting by herself at a table with a drink. She doesn't look thrilled to be there.

**You:** *<smile and walk over to her from a direction where she can see you coming>* Hi! How are you?

**Her:** *<asks you to repeat, then answers>* I'm good.

**You:** Oof, it is loud in here. I can barely hear you.

**Her:** It is making my ears ring.

**You:** Hey, you don't belong in here. This isn't what I like either. Let's get out of here. *<You offer her your hand to help her up from the table>*

**Her:** *<gives you a quick look>* Okay.

*<Reset the conversation in another direction as you two head elsewhere.>*

## NOTES AND OBSERVATIONS

If some sort of break or change is needed in the flow of your interaction, then maybe get her to move or take a walk with you. Here you had an unworkable environment for discussion. I have no problems with meeting people in bar settings, but they aren't for everyone. Your "let's get out of here" in this case was well received. Your gut and your read of her body language were telling you she was uncomfortable. She had probably already noticed you and was hoping you would come over. You took the lead and offered her another option. Sometimes a change of setting seems called for if for no other reason, to give her a break.

Another case where you might suggest you leave together right away is if she gets upset telling a story or talking about a family member or friend. If she is tearing up, it might be a good time to lead her to another, more private, place. That shows you have empathy and are listening.

## IN-PERSON | CONVERSATION 12

**SITUATION:** You are in a store and notice a pretty woman shopping for bug spray.

**You:** <*smile*> The bugs are crazy this year, huh?

**Her:** <*opens up immediately, totally comfortable with you*> <tells long story about bugs bothering people on a football field)

**You:** Hi, my name is <*first name*>

**Her:** I'm Jolene

**You:** That's a pretty name. I like it! <*You make reference to the Dolly Parton song coming out many years before her she was born, foretelling her glorious arrival.*>

**Her:** <*laughs, pretends to be offended, joking tone*> <*She says something flirty about that being a reference to her body, gesturing toward her ample chest*>

**You:** Yes, I was admiring how pretty you are, but in the nicest possible way. <*transition time here*> Hey, what are you up to today, apart from planning to get your revenge on these bugs?

**Her:** <*laughs*> Not too much.

**You:** There's a nice, mostly bug-free ice cream place nearby. Want to go over there after you're done here.

**Her:** Yeah, that sounds great. It's hot today!

## NOTES AND OBSERVATIONS

Oftentimes ladies, no matter what their age, say something sexual right off the bat. Please don't go down that path with her. Just use the opportunity to compliment her somehow like we did here, laugh and transition to something else. It might be tempting to get caught up talking about sexual topics, but you don't want her to start thinking you are getting overly fixated on sex with her. She knows you are interested. Keep talking to her like a normal human being. If she wants to show you how beautiful her body is, she can do that later in private. Feel free to let her know that you noticed, as in this case, but you are treating her like a person you are interested in first.

## IN-PERSON | CONVERSATION 13

**SITUATION:** You are at an outdoor arts and crafts event browsing the various displays. You notice a lady with an unusual necklace.

**You:** That color really complements your eyes. Stunning! And distracting, I forgot what I was doing. Hi, I'm <*first name*>.

**Her:** <*laughs*> I'm Ballentine.

**You:** That's lovely. Where did you get it?

**Her:** I make them.
<*a large bug flies around you two while you are talking*>
What was that?

**You:** I thought it was a helicopter.

**Her:** <*laughs*>

**You:** Hey, if we are about to be swarmed by bugs, let me get your number.

**Her:** How about my Instagram?

**You:** Sure. <*you exchange contact information*>

## NOTES AND OBSERVATIONS

This is a situational example. I mean you saw someone interesting, noticed something interesting in how she was dressed, and very nicely worked that to your advantage. Just like most people, she liked being complimented on what ended up being something she made. Right there, you have something to ask her more about. She sounds like an artist, has design skills, and a good sense of style. So, you have several ways to extend the conversation and learn more about her in the process.

Notice that she offered her Instagram account name instead of her phone number. You will see that quite often these days. The reason a lady might offer a social media account instead is that she might be hesitant to give out her phone number to someone until she trusts them more. Communicating through Instagram or many of the other social media services doesn't require having each other's phone numbers. So, it is a personal safety and privacy move, not an insult to or rejection of you. In fact, you might want to investigate using that approach yourself when you aren't 100% sure about a particular lady.

## IN-PERSON | CONVERSATION 14

**SITUATION:** You are at an outdoor sporting event on a sunny summer day. You notice an attractive lady. There are no apparent Ten Rule issues visible. You decide to introduce yourself.

**You:** <*smile*> Hi! How are you?

**Her:** <*smiles*> Hi! I'm great. How are you?

**You:** Who are you rooting for?

**Her:** Nobody. I'm here with some girlfriends. I'm not much into sports, but it is beautiful out today. I'd normally be home writing poetry.

**You:** Oh really! That's different. Tell me about that.

**Her:** Want to go for a walk?<*you walk with her around the facility and she tells you a long history of her love of poetry and her writing*><*you listen and continue the conversation, but feel it is time to try to close*>

**You:** Hey, let's get out of here. You want to get a drink?

**Her:** <*takes her sunglasses off, revealing insanely beautiful eyes*> The sun is beating me down. I should probably look for my girlfriends.

**You:** But how are you going to show me your poetry?

**Her:** We can get together later. Give me your number.

**You:** *<hand her your phone, and let her dial herself to capture your number>* It was nice meeting you. I'll call you. *<keep your word and call her a couple days later>*

## NOTES AND OBSERVATIONS

This is another common example of how these interactions can go. You have a pleasant conversation that is at risk of fizzling out after one or both of you tire. You go with, "But how are you going to show me your poetry?" despite her not having offered to show you anything. Your tone of voice in delivering that is playful, so it doesn't sound pushy. Another point I want to make is, if the conversation isn't going where you want, you might need to steer it in a direction that helps you find out if she is interested in taking another step toward eventual dating. Your "Hey, let's get out of here. You want to get a drink?" flopped, and she almost left. You recover by calling back to the passion for poetry and jokingly inviting yourself to something you were never invited to do. That was a risk, but it paid off. It depends on the situation, but sometimes I like asking for something by not using a question. You want to spend more time with her and her poetry writing seems to be her passion. However, you couldn't care less about poetry but want more time to learn about her. So, a poetry reading is likely in your future, but that is the price you have chosen to pay.

One last point I want to make before we move on is about keeping your word. If you say you are going to call her, then call. If you agree to meet her, then show up. If you need to cancel a date, tell her as soon as you know you won't make it. If you change your mind about a date with her, contact her to cancel. You don't need to tell her why. Remember Rule 4 from our Ten Rules about not doing or saying anything to make her feel bad about herself. We are gentlemen; we act honorably and keep our word.

## IN-PERSON | CONVERSATION 15

**SITUATION:** You are walking in the park, and notice a pretty woman eating lunch by herself. You decide to say hello.

**You:** Hi there! How are you?

**Her:** I'm good. What's up?

**You:** I just saw you over here, and decided to come say Hi. I'm *<first name>*.

**Her:** I'm Noelle.

**You:** nice to meet you. What are you up to today?

**Her:** *<she launches into several long stories about work, people she knows>*

**You:** *<you listen attentively, but are wondering when she will stop>* You have 60 points.

**Her:** *<pauses to process that, but it makes no sense>* Sorry?

**You:** I have been scoring and assigning points for your stories. I gave 10 points for A, 30 for B, and 10 apiece for the last two.

**Her:** *<is stunned, and pauses>*

**You:** Noelle, I think you are a very rare person. Let's get together later. I want to talk more. I think you are interesting. Can I get your number?

**Her:** Sure, we can text. Or email if you want.

**You:** I prefer speaking in person.

**Her:** Okay. *<gives you her phone to set up the contact information>*

## NOTES AND OBSERVATIONS

This will happen to you often, a very talkative woman. The way you ended her monologue was abrupt and unexpected, but you must move on after a certain amount of time. If you are still interested in her, you need to try to get her either a quick date or to exchanging contact information to arrange another meeting. Talking forever and ending up with nothing isn't a great use of your time.

The second point here is about what types of communication I think you should prefer. As I said elsewhere in the book, studies have shown anywhere from 80-90% of human communication happens through body language and tonality. The remaining 10-20% are the actual words you say. You steered her away from texting with you, not because she is a chatterbox, but because you want to use all 100% of the communication channels to learn more about each other.

## IN-PERSON | CONVERSATION 16

**SITUATION:** You are on vacation and staying in a hotel. Many people there are attending a conference on money laundering according to a sign in the lobby. You are coming down in the elevator with a pretty blond and some others wearing conference badges. You would like to meet her and, to make that happen, decide to provide an Oscar-worthy acting performance in the short time you have together on the elevator....

**You:** *<pretend to answer your phone>*
Yeah, yeah. Right. Just stage the money transfers like normal, but keep each between 8 and 9 thousand this time. That should stay under the radar.
*<pause> <make eye contact with her>*
Don't worry about that. Our guy at the embassy is good for another 8 months, and can squash any treaty requests.
*<to her, and pointing to your phone>*
Can you believe that?

**Her:** *<What you said sounds like money laundering to her. She looks shocked, and looks about to speak>*
*<pauses>* Do you know we are about to go to a money laundering conference?

**You:** What? Me too, but I thought it was *for* money launderers. To skill up. No? My bad!

**Her:** No!

**You:** <*big smile*> I kid. There was no call. Have you had breakfast? Let's go downstairs. Do you have time? They've got good coffee.

## NOTES AND OBSERVATIONS

This was a pretty big fake story. Take care to not get yourself arrested accidentally if the subject of your fake confession is actually a crime. It may be better to confine yourself to confessing to something harmless and funny-sounding. That reminds me of the Seinfeld episode where Jerry tells a woman he is the one behind the crop circles in England. His one-liner: *"You know, I'm the* one responsible for *those crop circles in England."*

## IN-PERSON | CONVERSATION 17

**SITUATION:** The use of props.

**You:** Hello there! How are you?

**Her:** Hi! I was just noticing your chain. What is that?

**You:** It's a shark's tooth. I've had this a while, I got it when I was in Asia.

**Her:** Oh wow! How was that?

*<Continue the conversation, but turn the questions back to her when the timing feels right.>*

### NOTES AND OBSERVATIONS

I am not a fan of being overly reliant on props for flirting, nor am I against their use. If you decide to carry or use props, you risk being one-dimensional. It is a matter of taste and personal style if you wear or carry conversation-starters, as in this example. Do whatever you are comfortable with, or just rely on your charm, wit, overall look, how you carry yourself, and your depth of character.

About how you answered her question, you gave he the literal answer and then a little more color to give her something to use as a hook to continue the exchange.

I have seen some masterclass-level use of props in my travels. For example, I recall being on a beach near Athens, Greece, and seeing a guy walking a tiny baby duck on a long, colorful string along the water. The cute little peeps from the fluffy yellow baby duck got people's attention. He would walk near the best-looking women so they can see the duck up close and he can gauge their reaction. He sometimes would put the duck on their bare bellies if they are lying face-up. He then would pour a tiny amount of water in the lady's belly button for the duck to drink from. Otherwise, he pours a small amount of water in her cupped hand and moves the bird in place to drink. That is some bold, high IQ prop usage there, as long as your duck doesn't get attacked by a dog and create a scene of horror.

If you are so inspired, you can use a puppy in a similar way at the beach, in a park, or on the street. Who doesn't want to cuddle a puppy? You can ask for the close by inviting her to the puppy's birthday party - the 3-month celebration of his glorious arrival! Who said a gentleman can't be bold? Not me. We have our rules, but we can be courageous as long as we adhere to our principles and are respectful of everyone.

## IN-PERSON | CONVERSATION 18

**SITUATION:** You are in a sports bar for a big game for your favorite team, and a lady in a mixed group of women and men catches your eye. She isn't alone. You don't know if she is with anyone else in her group. You suspect not, but position yourself near the group to try to strike up a conversation about the action in the game with anyone in the group.

**You:** *<you finally work your way through the group and can introduce yourself to her>* Hi there! Crisp jersey! I'm *<first name>*. Sorry, I didn't catch your name?

**Her:** Hi! Thank you! I just got this for today. I'm Kelly.

**You:** Can I get you a drink?

**Her:** Sure, I'm having _____ today. Thank you so much!

**You:** What's good on the menu here? The food.

**Her:** *<she tells you her opinion>*
<you stay near here for the rest of the game, casually chatting here and there. The game ends and people are packing up to leave>

**You:** That was fun. It was great meeting you. I'd like to see you later. Can I get your number?

**Her:** Sure.

## NOTES AND OBSERVATIONS

Remember, when the person you are interested in is in a group, don't go straight for her. Her husband or boyfriend could be one of the guys there. No matter what, always be respectful to everyone in the group as you try to figure out if she is available, and look for an opening to introduce yourself to her. Group settings are just different, but if you see someone you want to meet, you need to first navigate through the group correctly. If you go straight for her, an upset husband or boyfriend might jump in. Groups are just more complicated by their nature, but are a solvable problem as long as you have a plan, are observant and friendly, and show respect to everyone there.

Another point I want to make here is about expensive first dates. What happened here wasn't a date. You have her number, and you will call to try to arrange a meeting. Given the circumstances, it might be tempting to invite her to a live game or fan event. I caution you against doing anything expensive on the first few dates. Tickets for professional sporting events, or fan events where merchandise and autographs are sold, can be quite expensive. You are a generous guy with a big heart, but try to limit those early dates to free or cheap options. You don't know if she will cancel, or no-show, or not be a match. So, please consider not spending too much early on.

## IN-PERSON | CONVERSATION 19

**SITUATION:** You are driving and pull up alongside a pretty woman at a stop light. Her window is down, but her radio is playing loudly. You make eye contact and smile. You point to a parking lot in front of you. She nods yes, and pulls ahead of you. You both safely park off of the road in the parking lot.

**You:** *<you get out and walk to her car>* Hi! I'm not crazy. It is just your smile, and your eyes, and I could just feel your energy.

**Her:** *<laughs>* That's fine. *<she opens her door to get out>*

**You:** *<thinking of her sense of safety, you back away a little to give her room and not crowd her. She is a petite person, but looks like perfection from head to toe>*
Oh my gosh! I mean this is the nicest way. You look like a perfect combination of women's health and beauty.

**Her:** *<she tries to deflect that heavy compliment with humor>* My friends tell me I look like a porn star. Yeah, I'm the one they bring in when the Viagra doesn't work. *<laughs>*

**You:** *<uh-oh. And holy smoke! Laugh and change the subject>* You're hilarious! Look, thanks for stopping. I saw you and I knew I would regret it if we didn't meet. What are you up to today?

**Her:** I'm just running a few errands. You?

**You:** Oh, and I stopped you. Me too. Say, let me get your number. Let's get together for dinner or something when you are done.

**Her:** Sure, here. Text me.

**You:** Okay. Do you think you will be done around 4-5 PM?

**Her:** Yep

## NOTES AND OBSERVATIONS

Admire her beauty, but don't get hung up on her appearance or the super sexy and distracting thing she said. To this day I don't understand why, but some women like to bring up something highly sexual very early in these conversations. If it is a test, you will pass it with the mindset here, by following our process, and by strictly adhering to the Ten Rules. This stunning work of art has given you the gift of an opportunity to connect with her. You should do that because she sounds like she is fun, smart, and engaging. Plus, it was you that asked her to pull over in traffic.

## IN-PERSON | CONVERSATION 20

**SITUATION:** While shopping at your local grocery store, you see an extraordinarily pretty, artfully tattooed woman in a beautiful pink designer dress.

**You:** <*There are no obvious Ten Rule issues. You summon the courage to approach this stunner and walk over*> Sorry. Hi! You look like a beautiful work of art that came to life. I had to come over.

**Her:** <*she isn't smiling, but does make eye contact and responds flatly*> Hi.

**You:** <*you get a sense that she gets approached a lot because of her appearance, and doesn't like it*>
What are you up to today?

**Her:** Doing a little grocery shopping. <*she answers politely, but still isn't smiling*>

**You:** <*pause, thinking of what next to say*>

**Her:** <*her body language is showing lack of interest. She isn't looking at you now. She angled her body away from you where before you were facing each other directly*>

**You:** I am not sure where I am going with this, but that was 100% a compliment.

**You:** I'll be honest. There is just something about your energy that caught my eye. There is your whole look, your whole vibe, and I am not sure I am articulating it right.

**Her:** I am an artist at heart. Maybe that is it? But that doesn't pay the bills. <*laughs*> I'm not a great employee, so I just opened up a small makeup, hair and yoga place and am going through that stress now. That is a lot. There went my savings, and my credit card, and ... <*she smiles*>

**You:** <*try to recover using the first compliment that comes to mind relevant to what she just said, in what she hopefully hears in a playful but positive tone*> That's great you started your own business! I am picturing your mind as a beehive of activity. What may appear to be chaos to the untrained eye is really a system of order and productivity.

**Her:** <*bursts with:*> That's exactly right! <*laughs*>

**You:** <*smiling and laughing back*> ahhhh. That explains it. You look like the very picture of health.

**Her:** <*laughs*> <*She seems to relax and lower her guard after that risky, off-the-cuff "beehive brain" transition attempt from you. Now you two can talk more casually and see what happens from there. You now have several ways you can go in the conversation by asking about her business and her passion around women's beauty or health. If everything feels right, work toward closing by getting her contact information.*>

## NOTES AND OBSERVATIONS

Not every approach goes well. That is just a fact. Any dating books, videos, coaches, or training classes that tell you they have an 80, 90, or nearly 100% success rate are lying to you. The real world doesn't work that way. This example covers something you will undoubtedly encounter in real world approaches – a lady who is reluctant to lower her guard. In every approach, you need to be listening to what she is saying, how she is saying it, and pay attention to her body language to understand how things are going.

Here we have a stunningly beautiful lady that probably draws a lot of unwanted attention every day due to her highly attractive appearance. Her guard is understandably always up. Your first two opener attempts didn't work at all, and she seemed to be giving you signals that meant "go away". You respectfully tried one more thing to try to start down the path of making sure that she knows you aren't interested in her merely for her appearance or for sex. You tried to show that you are interested in her as a person and that you are someone she can trust at all times and in all situations. You rolled the dice with a risky attempt to transition the conversation (the beehive brain comment), and she liked it. You never know what will work, but she is smart and had a great sense of humor about it after you got past her defenses. Remember, you aren't trying to trick her or force her to lower those defenses. You want her to trust you enough to want to naturally lower her defenses.

## IN-PERSON | CONVERSATION 21

**SITUATION:** You enter an auto repair shop waiting room as your vehicle is being serviced. The room has maybe 5 people in it, but can seat 60 comfortably. The people already there are spread about as far apart as the space allows. As you look around, you see a pretty woman seated there. What do you do?

**You:** *<you're feeling social, and the pretty woman already there seems to be a good choice, if she is up for it. You walk over near her, point to a chair two spots away from her, and ask if it is taken>*

**Her:** *<smiles>* No, go ahead.

**You:** Thank you! Hi! How are you?

**Her:** Hi!

**You:** How is your patient doing? *<assuming she has a car there being worked on>*

**Her:** Oh my god! *<goes into a story about mechanical problems with her car, and the costs>*

**You:** I'm so sorry. Normally this brand doesn't give a lot of trouble. *<smiles>* Thank goodness you are wealthy!

**Her:** What? Hardly *<laughs>* I work as a visiting nurse. And I am in ballet.

**You:** *<you now have two great subjects to drill in to, both of which you are genuinely interested in learning more about from her><She seems to like talking. You have a long conversation about both subjects, and enjoyed every minute of it.>*

<After a while, the service manager comes and tells you your car is ready, but not hers yet>

**You:** I'm so sorry, I get to go first, *<laughs>* First, I want to thank you for pouring your soul into being such a great occupation—physical therapist—and helping people. Second thing *<pause briefly and smile>* Can I get your number?

**Her:** Sure!

## NOTES AND OBSERVATIONS

In this example, you are helping the universe along by stacking the deck in your favor. You could have easily sat anywhere in that vast waiting room, but you wanted to try to strike up a conversation with the one pretty woman there. That isn't creepy, not in the perfectly respectful and fun way you will try it. If she isn't receptive to the interaction, you will immediately stop. Your other option is to sit far away from everyone and regret never trying to speak to her. You pick Option 1, and it pays off. This is another example of how pretty much the entire world is your flirting zone, not just bars, parties, and nightclubs.

## IN-PERSON | CONVERSATION 22

**SITUATION:** You are walking in your neighborhood and cross paths with a lady you would like to meet.

**You:** (smile and make eye contact> Hi! How are you?

**Her:** *<smiles>* Hi!

**You:** I don't think we've met, but I've seen you around, I think. Do you live around here?

**Her:** Yeah, I'm right over there. I think I have seen you? I moved in a couple months ago.

**You:** I am just one block over. Oh wait, three blocks over. Wow, you are so pretty, I got disoriented.

**Her:** At least it's my fault for a good reason with a *<laughs>*

**You:** You know what, if you are free this weekend, there is a Greek Festival both days. Let's get together and check that out.

**Her:** Yeah. Sure, that sounds fun.

**You:** Great! *<hand her your phone>* Give me your number and we can sort out the time.

## NOTES AND OBSERVATIONS

Always be on the lookout for interesting local events, shows, festivals, and restaurants to bring a date to. Having interesting date ideas already in mind comes in handy in cases like this. Again, I strongly suggest you limit the first date or two to either cheap or free activities. In this case, you picked a food festival that you know is good and doesn't empty out your wallet. I am not endorsing being cheap. I think it is best practice to cap your expenses on first dates because they so often disappoint. You don't want it to be too expensive of a disappointment.

## IN-PERSON | CONVERSATION 23

**SITUATION:** You are out shopping for Christmas decorations. A pretty lady comes nearby and catches your attention.

**You:** *<she is looking at artificial trees>* I can't believe how low the prices on these Christmas trees. I have a hard time figuring out how they can be made, shipped, and sold for profit at that price.

**Her:** Yeah. But these are kinda plain. *<She takes a nearby little cheap-looking fake flower tree topper and puts it on one of display trees>*

**You:** That's what was missing! That was a masterclass-quality demonstration of your design skills! They're really going to fly off the shelves now!

**Her:** Yeah, I've still got it. *<laughs>* Funny you should say that, I went to four years of art school. Not that I am using it, but I have the degree *<laughs>*

**You:** Could've fooled me. If I may ask, what do you do now? *<The ice is broken now. You can ask a few questions and go back-and-forth with her to see if there is any chemistry, and if so, work toward whatever close makes sense under the circumstances>*

## NOTES AND OBSERVATIONS

Here is another situational example. Honestly, some ladies are so pretty that you have to take a chance. Doing nothing isn't an option sometimes as long as there are no Ten Rules issues. You were in the Christmas section of a store anyway, so you went for what was in front of you for subject matter for a playful interaction. The over-the-top joking about her design skills could have flopped or backfired, but that was a risk worth taking. I wouldn't keep calling back to the opener. I would rather use this opportunity to talk about her, and if she is interested, she will ask about you. A natural human-to-human conversation is what you want to see if there is any chemistry there, and to confirm her availability to ask for some sort of close (contact information or immediate date).

## IN-PERSON | CONVERSATION 24

**SITUATION:** You are standing curbside on a street waiting to uber home. You notice a lady waiting at the bus stop with a shirt that says "Sasshole" on it. Curiosity gets the best of you…

**You:** Is that your design there? *<you ask jokingly, pointing to your chest instead of hers and smiling>*

**Her:** *<smiles>* A client made it for me.

**You:** Oh. May I ask what business are you in?

**Her:** *<tells her story, including the full lore behind "Sasshole"> <Voila! Another natural conversation quickly materializes out of thin air. See where that goes, and either close or exit. Either way she will be leaving feeling great about the interaction, which is in accordance with Rule 4.>*

### NOTES AND OBSERVATIONS

Be fearless. Most people don't mind being asked about some interesting article of clothing they are wearing or an eye-catching accessory they have on. She is wearing a shirt that says "Sasshole" for a reason. She probably has a great sense of humor. The "Sasshole" shirt alone gives you a way to enter a conversation with her. Take the opportunity if you feel drawn to her!

## IN-PERSON | CONVERSATION 25

**SITUATION:** You are out for a thrilling day of bath towel shopping.

**You:** *<to a nearby lady who seems to work in the store>* Hi Pretty! Do you know if you have – I am not sure what to call them - any luxury towels? I stayed in a nice hotel for work recently, and I'd love to find similar towels for my house.

**Her:** *<she perks up on the surprise "Hi Pretty">* Most guys who come in here for new towels or bedsheets have just gotten a new girlfriend.

**You:** What? *<smile>* would I lie to you, ... *<then you try to read her name and stop>*

**Her:** *<points to her name badge>* Can you say my name? *<smiles>*

**You:** Of course I can. Come here and show me. *<It is some exotic name that you know will come out as gibberish. You try anyway, undeterred by this flirty woman. With exaggerated confidence, you badly mispronounce her name>* How perfectly did I do? I probably pronounced it better than anyone ever, apart from you.

**Her:** You're funny! It is *<name pronounced correctly>*

**You:** That's lovely. Hey, we need to work on getting me to say your name correctly. You should help me with that. When do you get off work?

**Her:** In a couple hours.

**You:** Give me your number. Text me when you are done and ready to go.

**Her:** Ummm. Sure, okay. We can do that.

<*You exchange numbers and finalize the details. She gives you her phone to enter your number. Before you give it back, send yourself a text message from her saying how handsome you are with a winking emoji.*>

## NOTES AND OBSERVATIONS

Your honest and well-intentioned attempt to buy new towels ultimately failed, but at least you got a date out of it. I don't suggest flirting with people at their work too much, apart from getting a quick phone number here and there. They are there to work, but she started in with you, and that renders you blameless. Still, don't spend a lot of time keeping her from her work. Steer her toward meeting in your free time. Reply to the text from her phone (to the message that was really from you), thanking her for the compliment and telling her you couldn't help noticing how pretty she was too. That's a corny trick, but she will likely think it is cute.

## IN-PERSON | CONVERSATION 26

**SITUATION:** You are out for a walk and see what seems like a 10 out of 10 appearance-wise coming toward you. She looks like a piece of art has come to life.

**You:** Miss, you're pushing the bar up pretty high up on the 10 scale, aren't you? Is that fair to the other ladies?

**Her:** Excuse me? *<she says smiling>*

**You:** You look like perfection in every detail (health, beauty, style) from what I can see. I was just wondering if that is fair to other ladies around.

**Her:** Wow!! Oh, well, that's their problem. *<laughs>*

**You:** *<you should now transition away from the subject of her appearance>* I guess the world will always have some injustices. For instance, I'm probably the best boyfriend material in the city, and maybe of all time. That's isn't fair either.

**Her:** Oh really? Do tell! *<smiles>*

**You:** That would take me a month just for the backstory. Nah, I'm just kidding. I'd like to get to know you a bit. Let's go grab some coffee. Do you want some coffee or tea?

**Her:** Yeah. I could go for that.

## NOTES AND OBSERVATIONS

Women at certain levels of attractiveness have been told they are pretty in plain language multiple times per day for their entire life. You come in using something she has never heard before. Yes, this could easily backfire. She has likely already heard everything, so gambling on a longshot approach with confidence and flair maybe isn't a bad idea. No risk, no reward.

## IN-PERSON | CONVERSATION 27

**SITUATION:** Lady is straightening shelves in a bookstore

**You:** It looks like a never-ending chore, reorganizing all of that.

**Her:** *<laughs>* Yes

**You:** I apologize on behalf of all of us Neanderthals that keep messing up your work like that.

**Her:** *<laughs>* It gives me something to do to pass the time

**You:** *<needing an extender try:>* If I worked here, I would get fired for sneaking off in a corner somewhere and reading books from cover to cover. I have been a voracious reader since I can remember. Bookstores and libraries draw me in.

**Her:** Same here. I do that sometime, sneak off on a break and read a while.

**You:** Oh yeah? What are you in to, what do you read?

**Her:** *<rattles off her list of interests>*

**You:** I like A and B as well. I don't want to hold you up here at work. Let's get together some time.

**Her:** Yeah, okay.

**You:** Let me get your number.

### NOTES AND OBSERVATIONS

After that brief exchange, she hopefully thinks of you as bold, funny, intelligent, and interesting. You succeeded in getting her number. Keep your word and call her to set up a time to meet outside of her work.

## IN-PERSON | CONVERSATION 28

**SITUATION:** She sits down right next to you on the subway and starts rummaging through her purse.

**You:** < *Looking at her overloaded purse*> It looks like you have one of everything in there.

**Her:** <*smiles*> I do. That is why I need the big bag.

**You:** Maybe I should carry around a bag? But I don't have much that won't fit in a pocket or two.

**Her:** I should restrict myself to a pocket or two. <*She then starts showing you the various things she has in her bag that she says she cannot be without*>

**You:** From my seat, I don't think you need a lick of that make-up. You have this wonderful mix of health and women's beauty going on. I don't think you need anything. Red ink on a rose.

**Her:** Whew! I'm blushing over here. You haven't seen me without makeup.

**You:** I'd like to sometime. This is my stop coming up. <*you give her a contact card*> Here you go. Can I get your number? My information is on the card.

**Her:** Sure

## NOTES AND OBSERVATIONS

You didn't have much to go on, nor do you have much time to act. You don't need to always start the same way. Situational openers can work fine. Consider carrying a few contact cards around for when your phones might not work have service, you are in a hurry, or the other person doesn't have a working smartphone on them.

## IN-PERSON | CONVERSATION 29

**SITUATION:** You are out and about in public, and she is wearing a struggling sports team's jersey

**You:** Short on joy this season, huh? *<smile and point to her shirt>*

**Her:** Oh my god! My Dad. My brothers are all complaining. *<laughs>*

**You:** I think it is okay to have a secret, backup team for times like this. You don't have to tell anybody. What do you think?

**Her:** I do, sort of. I like one or two players on every team. We have a new local chapter of the fan club here. We meet at a restaurant every game day. You should check it out. The food is good there and we get our own private area.

**You:** Sign me up! *<smile>* I'll check that out. Hey, let me get your number.

**Her:** Sure.

## NOTES AND OBSERVATIONS

I like in-person openers that are bold, that use as few words as possible, and are humorous and unique. This one ticks all those boxes.

"What do you think?" is a good conversation extender. She solved the problem of moving toward a close for you due to your shared interest. This exchange didn't help you learn much about her, but you have her phone number to try again. And you can consider attending the fan club event that she mentioned and look her up in person there.

## IN-PERSON | CONVERSATION 30

**SITUATION:** You are out on the walking at a local park getting some fresh air. You awkwardly cross paths more than once with the same attractive lady, and decide to explain why you didn't speak up earlier.

**You:** <*make eye contact and smile*> Hi! I wanted to say hi to you earlier, but I was fighting off a sneeze.

**Her:** <*laughs*> okay!

**You:** I wanted to put some distance between us in case I lost.

**Her:** I appreciate that! Are you okay now?

**You:** I've pulled myself together. <*smile*> I'm <*first name*>. How are you?

**Her:** <*laughs*> Hi, I'm Megan.

**You:** Nice to meet you, Megan. <*extender needed at this point*> What are you up to today?

**Her:** Just out getting some sun. You?

**You:** Fresh air and a walk. Want to walk together?

**Her:** Sure. Let's go!

*<Who said this had to be difficult? Now, what do you do? Ask her about herself. What is her typical day like? What does she do for a living? Where else does she go when she needs to take a break? Listen carefully to everything she tells you and build on whatever parts interest you. Be prepared for her to reflect the same or similar questions back to you.>*

## NOTES AND OBSERVATIONS

The opener here is bizarre and unexpected. It was designed to surprise her. Many women like men who are fine by themselves and who are, by flirting with them, merely inviting her to share time together. Those ladies are impressed, ironically enough, that the guy doesn't care if she says no. He doesn't care because he knows if she says no, the next lady likely will say yes. In this example, your opener sends that subtle message. You can be weird, but are also fun and interesting to be with.

## IN-PERSON | CONVERSATION 31

**SITUATION:** As you are heading toward the cashier area of a store, you notice a petite lady looking like she is dreading trying to hoist heavy bags of dog food into her shopping cart.

**You:** Hey, let me get that for you. I need the karma points.

**Her:** Ohhh. Thank you!

**You:** Move the bread. I don't want to crush anything. Do you need another bag?

**Her:** No, thanks! I don't think you need any karma points. *<her tone suggests that is meant as a flirt and a compliment>*

**You:** I like to run up the score just in case. When I get a chance, I step in. *<pause>* I promise I didn't come over here to hit on you, but you have the prettiest eyes!

**Her:** So do you.

**You:** Thanks! I think I am pretty ordinary looking guy though.

**Her:** *<looks you straight in the eyes>* You have to know where to look.

**You:** *<holy crap!>* Hey, I'd like to get to know you a bit. How can we do that?

**Her:** I need to feed my starving dog. How about we exchange numbers, and we can go from there?

**You:** Sounds good.

## NOTES AND OBSERVATIONS

Stepping in to help a someone in need is a good opener on its own. As for moving the conversation past lifting the heavy bags, people like to be complimented on their eyes. It is a good one to go for to tell her you find her attractive without being creepy by talking about her body or something sexual. Her "you have to know where to look" while looking you in the eyes is a deep and incredibly impactful comeback to use when one party is disparaging their own appearance. Jot that one down.

## IN-PERSON | CONVERSATION 32

**SITUATION:** You are passing time in a department store shopping for crisp new additions to your wardrobe, when you notice a lady trying on shoes and carefully examining how she looks in each pair in a mirror.

**You:** You look good in everything. I think it is more you make the items look good than the other way around.

**Her:** *<surprised look><laughs>* Thank you!

**You:** I need to start coming to this store more often.

**Her:** Why is that?

**You:** I was wondering where the hotties shop around here. *<now immediately defuse that heavy compliment>* I get most of my stuff online.

**Her:** I buy a lot online, as much as I can these days.

**You:** Come over and help me pick out some shirts when you are done. I'd like help with the colors, if you have time.

**Her:** I don't work here, but alright!

**You:** This place is huge. Give me your number in case we cannot find each other.

**Her:** *<she pulls her phone out of her bra>*

**You:** *<You say with the tone of a man with the quiet confidence to ask what you are about to ask her>* What else do you keep in there? *<give her your phone to type her number in>*

**Her:** *<laughs>* Are you on Insta or Snap?

**You:** Yeah, I'll send that to you. See you in a little bit!

**Her:** Okay.

## NOTES AND OBSERVATIONS

The opener here is an unexpected and creatively-constructed compliment. That type of opener should go over well with most women. Later asking her for help with your shopping is the truly bold part. It paid off in this case. You can use that time with her later to learn more about her and see if there is any chemistry. If not, at least you have some fun, and from a practical point of view, you get a stylish woman's opinion on what colors truly look best on you.

## IN-PERSON | CONVERSATION 33

**SITUATION:** A single woman you are interested in meeting lives in your apartment complex. You leave a few minutes early each day to scrape the ice and snow from her windshield, taking extreme caution not to scratch or damage her car.

**You:** *<put your work in without expecting a word of thanks>*

**Her:** *<eventually she makes a point of looking to see who is clearing her car windows on bad winter days, and recognizes you. One day, she comes out to thank you>*
Hi! Thank you so much for doing that! I HATE scraping ice and snow.

**You:** It's my pleasure. Hey, I'm *<first name>*.
*<Don't mention why you have been doing this. She knows why. You wanted to meet her. Your opening move just was the longest in history, spanning days or weeks>*

**Her:** I'm Heather.

**You:** Heather, it's nice to meet you! It's been so cold. Hey, I'm having some people over Saturday for barbecue and chili. You should come over. Do you eat that kind of stuff? If not, I'll pick up something for you.

**Her:** Oh no. I love meat. What time should I come over, and what can I bring? I don't want to come empty-handed.
*<laughs>*

## NOTES AND OBSERVATIONS

Who said your opener had to consist of words at all? Also, your being able to cook is, to women, a useful and highly sought-after skill.

## IN-PERSON | CONVERSATION 34

**SITUATION:** The lady at the table next to you in a coffee shop pulls out one of those fully-featured day planner binder things.

**You:** You are impressively organized.

**Her:** Yeah, I like to be an organized person.

**You:** What do you do? I'm guessing accountant or lawyer or CEO of something.

**Her:** I'm working my way through school. I got a late start, but I am getting there! <*smiles*>

**You:** Ahh, good for you! Studying what? To what end, if I may ask?

**Her:** I want to be a veterinarian. What do you do?

**You:** That's great! <*you know how several directions the conversation can do as you decide if you want to get to a close*>

## NOTES AND OBSERVATIONS

That's an excellent and compact situational opener. There are probably thousands of possible situational openers, so I cannot possibly cover every type here. If you like using those, keep your subject matter and your wording 100% positive. Here, instead of a plain "that's a nice binder" you went for "you look impressively organized". See the difference? Look for something good to say about her, the environment around you, or the situation you are in. Don't let anything you say, even when joking, sound critical of her or negative. Bring that extra pop of positive energy from the very start of your interaction with her, and continue pouring on the energy at a reasonable level throughout. Being average might not be good enough.

## IN-PERSON | CONVERSATION 35

**SITUATION:** You are at the downtown city center walking around to see what's new. She's walking alone. You see no rings or signs of trouble.

**You:** Sorry, I was trying not to look too much. I didn't want to come off as staring or creepy. I was admiring every detail of your look. You're pretty, obviously, right. But your styling. The colors. Everything. You look camera-ready. I didn't mean it to be too much. I just wanted to soak it all in.

**Her:** That's OK. You're fine. You can tell when someone is sincere.

**You:** I was just walking around to see what is new. It's been a while since I came downtown. Want to go for a walk?

**Her:** Sure.

**You:** What brings you here today?
*<Have your standard, natural, human-to-human conversation with her. Use our mental trick if need be and think of her as a long-time friend you are just catching up with. What would you ask such a person? What are they doing these days? How are they doing? Look for interesting hooks in what she says to ask more, to find out more about her. If the chemistry is there, ask her for coffee or a drink right now, or get her contact information to arrange something for later>*

## NOTES AND OBSERVATIONS

She has made quite an effort to look great from head to toe, and when you see that, oftentimes compliments are appreciated. Ladies aren't out to be judged by every passing person, but if your tone, wording, and body language are all positive, non-aggressive, non-sexual, and sincere, it should be well-received. She knows you are attracted to her, but you told her about it in a good way. Then you proceeded to talk to her like a normal human being to get to know her. We gentlemen don't need pickup artist tricks or lines. It isn't the crispy delivery of some memorized line that is going to help you meet that great lady you want; it is being a good man with good intentions. It is you being prepared, and you improving yourself every day to be the man she will later think is the greatest partner/husband/father on the planet.

## IN-PERSON | CONVERSATION 36

**SITUATION:** You go to the beach to soak up some sun and enjoy the day while getting some reading done for work. You placed yourself on a towel a respectful distance from the prettiest women on the beach, because getting work done is more pleasant when the view is good.

**You:** *<you see a vendor selling flavored ice> <you walk over to the lady you like the most>* Hey, if someone messes with my stuff, pounce on them. Pound them good until I get back, with sand flying in the air and the whole works *<point to you stuff>* OK?

**Her:** Alright. I'll do it!

**You:** I'm going over to get one of those ice things from the guy over there. Can I bring you back something?

**Her:** No thanks! I have my water. I'm fine.

**You:** *<later, you return with your treat>* Mmmmm. This is good. Thanks for watching my stuff. You know, I'm working on some science stuff for NASA for a manned mission to Uranus. The planet. I can't talk about that much. You've done your country a great service in helping protect that vital work. *<smile>* You should be proud of that.

**Her:** *<smiles>* "Science stuff"? You wouldn't lie to me, would you?

**You:** Only if it was convenient...

**Her:** <*laughs*> Do I get a medal?

**You:** Yeah. Yeah, that can happen. I'll have to make a medal, but that can happen. Sure. I'll escort you to the medal ceremony. Give me your number and my people will contact your people.

**Her:** <*laughs*> OK. We'll see where this goes!

## NOTES AND OBSERVATIONS

This is a different way to enlist a stranger's services in a playful way as an opener. Giving a pretty woman a task to do on your behalf is fun. You have the confidence and audacity with this scheme to not even say hi. Later, to mix things up, there is intentionally lowbrow, schoolboy humor in the NASA joke. You don't know where the limits are sometimes until you cross them. We gentlemen are allowed to joke as long as we stay within the box of acceptable behavior for being respectful and appropriate. So, you give it a try to read her reaction. That goes well, and you play off her response to attempt to close.

## IN-PERSON | CONVERSATION 37

**SITUATION:** You are shopping in a builder's supply store for yourself. You come across a lovely woman sifting through the trim options in the wooden flooring section.

**You:** It is hard to find matches for those, huh?

**Her:** Everything is close, but not quite.

**You:** I see why folks recommend always buying extra and saving it. Extra tile, extra shingles, extra everything. It is almost impossible to find matches years later.

**Her:** I don't have any spares. I just bought an older house. I'm about to give up. *<smiles>*

**You:** I hope I am not being too forward, but you have the prettiest eyes.

**Her:** You think so? *<she turns to face you>* What color do you think they are?

**You:** *<lean in a bit for a closer look>* Hmmmmm. I see a blue-green. Mostly blue. Like a Walmart bag. Yes, "Walmart bag blue" I would say.

**Her:** *<frowns playfully at your lackluster description>*

**You:** How am I doing with the flirting?

**Her:** Not so good *<laughs>*

**You:** I can do better than this. I'll get it together.

**Her:** *<smiles, and maintains eye contact>*

**You:** Let's swap numbers, and we'll start over.

**Her:** Haha! That sounds good.

## NOTES AND OBSERVATIONS

Even if you don't get traction in the brief time you had for the opener, consider admitting that it didn't go well and ask her for another shot as the date request. Lemons to lemonade. She sees you are confident enough to approach her, yet still polite and respectful. And you have a sense of humor. Nothing about her body language or what she has said so far is showing signs she isn't receptive to you. So, be bold! Go for a close to see what happens.

## IN-PERSON | CONVERSATION 38

**SITUATION:** You are out to pick up a birthday card for a friend. You see someone interesting in the wedding card section.

**You:** Do they have any that tactfully say you are making a big mistake?

**Her:** <*laughs*> Don't get me started on that subject!

**You:** <*laugh*><*continue looking for the best card for your friend*>

**Her:** <*amazingly, she finds a card that has the level of snark you asked for, and she walks it over to you beaming with pride in her accomplishment*>

**You:** What's this? I cannot believe you found that! You must be the best rare item finder in the world!

**Her:** Anything else I can locate for you sir?

**You:** Well, my ferret just graduated from ninja school. Do you think they have a card for that?

**Her:** You're funny!

**You:** You're funny! Say, uh, what are you doing after this? What time is it?

**Her:** I was heading home. This was the major task for the day. I am off work today and tomorrow.

*<Complete the close. Since she has already offered up her days of availability, make firm plans to do something and get her contact information to coordinate the meeting.>*

## NOTES AND OBSERVATIONS

In your closes, try not to end up with some vague, wishy-washy plan. If you can, make firm plans. That is, if you cannot talk her into to coffee, a walk, or something easy right on the spot. Saying "How about dinner tomorrow at 7PM at restaurant name on street name" is far better than, let's "sort it out over text". Invest the time and make solid, detailed plans to do something that you will each think is fun and will look forward to. Being able to come up with great ideas on the spot like this is why I strongly recommend keeping careful track of the best places to go and fun things to do in your area.

## IN-PERSON | CONVERSATION 39

**SITUATION:** It is your first time at a massive combination horse racetrack, casino, and hotel complex. You are walking around it, seeing where everything is, and checking out the scenery. You notice a very pretty woman who seems to be doing the same thing. At one point, she pauses at the entryway of one portion of the facility and looks like she is trying to decide where to head next.

**You:** *<smoothly catch up to her and stand next to her, also looking around>* It's not even close, in case you are wondering.

**Her:** Sorry? I didn't catch that.

**You:** This is my first time here, and I've walked all over this facility to see what all they have. You are by far the best-looking woman here. And the interesting thing is *how* much prettier you are. You are without rival.

**Her:** *<looks equally happy and shocked, all at the same time>* *<She immediately offers her hand to shake yours and says with emphasis on each word>* Hi, I'm Amanda!

**You:** *<shake her hand>* I'm *<first name>*. I am pleased to meet you, Amanda. Are you with someone? *<point to bar across the hall>* Would you like to grab a drink with me?

**Her:** Sure *<laughs>*
*<and off you two go…>*

## NOTES AND OBSERVATIONS

Shock-and-awe works sometimes. But make sure you mean it if you are going all-out on complimenting someone like that. A lady who isn't confident in her appearance might think you are mocking her in some way. If you want to use this one, please practice your tone of voice beforehand. Deepen your voice, and speak slowly. That should help sell it with her. You cannot predict how she reacts to such a strong opener, but that is part of the fun of flirting!

## IN-PERSON | CONVERSATION 40

**SITUATION:** You are in the waiting room at your dentist. She is seated a few chairs away from you, tapping away at her phone. You've finished browsing the entire internet on your phone as you wait, and the magazine selection doesn't look great. You decide it's time to mingle...

**You:** Do you think the doctor's office magazine subscription market has plummeted with the advent of smartphones.

**Her:** *<smiles and looks up>* Yeah, that probably hasn't been great in years. The world keeps changing I guess.

**You:** If I my ask, what do you do for work?

**Her:** I am a police officer.

**You:** Oh wow! I'd better behave! I really appreciate what you do. You must have some wild stories. What is the third craziest thing you have seen?

**Her:** Third craziest? Not number one? Hmmmm. *<she then goes into that story, and then continues into her background and history a lot more>*
*<The dental assistant calls her in>*

**You:** Hey, let me get your phone number?

**Her:** Sure. *<scribbles it on a card and hands it over>*

## NOTES AND OBSERVATIONS

Some ladies are just waiting to open up to you. If she senses you are a good person with good intentions, the dam can just burst wide open. There might be something going on in society where people who want to talk to others in the classic, in-person way don't get many chances. People are on their phones or texting, or just don't speak up. Discussions are far more rich in person.

You can ask someone who really loves to talk something as simple as "how are you", and they might let loose with what feels like their life story. There are good points to that for your purposes, especially when you are first meeting someone:

1. You don't need to make much effort to lead the conversation,
2. She is telling you pretty much everything about her without you having to ask bit-by-bit and
3. You have plenty of hooks to use to ask her more about the things she mentioned that are of interest to you.

## IN-PERSON | CONVERSATION 41

**SITUATION:** You enter a coffee shop. There is a stunning woman waiting to pick up her order.

**You:** Hi! Can I ask you, what is the healthiest drink option in here that tastes good, and I will like, and has a kick to it.

**Her:** A coffee you mean?

**You:** Yes.

**Her:** Get the Americano. That is what I get. You'll like it.

*<You go to order exactly that, and get asked if you want it hot or cold><you look over to her and she has been following your progress, and tells the order-taker you want it cold>*
*<You pay, and rejoin her in the waiting area>*

**You:** Hey thanks! They're busy today.

**Her:** Yeah, they're good. I've been here a while. I can't stand too long.

**You:** Is it the heels? I am glad I am a guy and don't have to deal with ladies' dress shoes.

**Her:** *<smiles>* No. I am a dancer, and my body has paid a price for that. I dance and also practice ballet. I have been told my posture is too good, and that messed me up.

**You:** <*glance over and notice nothing wrong*> I am no expert, but your posture looks picture-perfect.

**Her:** I know it looks that way.

**You:** Hey, a table is open over there. Let's grab that.

**Her:** Yeah, I'll go reserve that for us. Here, grab my order please.

## NOTES AND OBSERVATIONS

Your opening question is intentionally unfair and unanswerable, but she gives it a try. There are good people all around you who want to help if you ask. You are just playing around with that fact. Right now, she doesn't know if that was an honest question or a guy flirting with her. The truth in this case is: both.

Places like coffee shops can be great spots for meeting people. Remember, with the tools in this book, pretty much the entire surface of the earth is your flirting zone. That includes up in the air, at sea, or any other place your find yourself apart from work, and maybe funerals, disaster areas, and active crime scenes. What is vital to your success with meeting great women is following our process for continuously making yourself a better man each day and strictly adhering to our Ten Rules and advice throughout this book.

## IN-PERSON | CONVERSATION 42

**SITUATION:** You are waiting to go across a pedestrian crosswalk to get to your car, but cars are whizzing past left and right. Two ladies walk up alongside you, and the cars quickly stop to let them pass.

**You:** You know, I only got to cross at this crosswalk because you pretty ladies showed up. If you hadn't, I would still be standing there.

**Her:** *<both ladies laugh. One of them says>* Thank you! My husband thinks so. But she is single. Are you married?

**You:** *<Dang! You have met your match for bold openers>* *<smile>* Yes, I'm single.

**Her:** Here. Give me your phone. I'm giving you her number *<laughs>*

**Her sister:** *<shrieks>* Oh my god! You are terrible! *<However, she makes no effort to prevent the exchange of phone numbers>*

**You:** *<to the sister>* With your permission, I'd like to call you.

**Her sister:** *<meekly>* Sure, that would be fine.

## NOTES AND OBSERVATIONS

If you carry yourself well and look your best, it won't always be you making the initial advance. Yes, you flirted at the crosswalk, but you do that sort of thing 24/7. Sometimes, whether you want to or not or you spoke to her first, a lady will approach you. Ladies, or their family members or friends who feel they have an eye for quality guys, can be quite bold about it.

This will happen to you as your confidence soars as you keep improving yourself every day. You stack those wins toward your goals every day to position yourself to be as strong of an asset as possible to the people you care most about in life. People can feel that growing, positive energy pumping from your chest. They can see it in how you talk, walk, and the effect you have when you enter a room. Some ladies will act on that feeling they are sensing about you, just as you do when you feel attracted to someone.

## IN-PERSON | CONVERSATION 43

**SITUATION:** You are picking up a few items for yourself in the local grocery store. You see a beauty with just a few vegetables in her basket.

**You:** *<point to her basket's contents>* Is that the kind of stuff I should be buying, instead of these treats and wandering the bakery aisle?

**Her:** *<She surveys what you are holding>* Well, I like those *<smiles, and points to a bag of chips>*

**You:** I never learned much about healthy eating when I was coming up. I never learned to like the taste of most vegetables. I grew up in the South, and sure, my mother fed us fried tobacco like most kids, but I was ever that fond of vegetables…

**Her:** Nooooo! Who fries tobacco? *<laughs>*

**You:** *<let that one simmer>* Oh. By the way, one of the cashiers here told me they have a healthy ice cream now. She said they sell it here.

**Her:** Healthy ice cream? I need to see that for myself.

*<You two walk over to the frozen foods. On the way, very casually ask her about herself and her background, drawing on her health*

*and wellness knowledge. You arrive at the ice cream section and, to your disappointment, there is no healthy ice cream there>*

**You:** I am not seeing anything. *<you weren't lying about this part, unlike the fried tobacco thing. You were told about healthy ice cream>*

**Her:** Me either.

**You:** Hmmm. Have I have been deceived? Deceived? Duped? Hoodwinked?

**Her:** *<laughs>*

**You:** Once again, healthy eating is just hard.

**Her:** Not really. I have some recipes.

**You:** I'd love to learn that. I am really struggling with this.

**Her:** Here, take my number...
*<and there you go>*

**NOTES AND OBSERVATIONS**

Whoever said that your flirting activities couldn't be educational and result in a possible health and wellness breakthrough for you? Looking at it more broadly, even when things don't work out with someone, you can learn a lot from loads of interesting people as you meet folks and date around over the coming weeks and months. This naturally works out well whether you are an introvert or an extrovert. Even if you are shy now, you will see as time goes on, talking to people you have never met will come to you as naturally as breathing. You will be able to arrange as many dates for yourself as you want.

## IN-PERSON | CONVERSATION 44

**SITUATION:** As you enter a convenience store to grab a drink, you notice a pretty woman standing at the spinning display where they cook the greasy hot dogs all day.

**You:** Don't do that to yourself. I can offer you an upgrade over those hot dogs.

**Her:** *<smiles, but says nothing>*

**You:** I mean, if you aren't thrilled with your options, I'd be happy to take you somewhere else. Your choice. My treat.

**Her:** I can't afford much more, I am on a budget. My restaurant closed up, and I need to find another job.

**You:** Oh, I'm sorry about that. I am sure you'll be fine. My offer stands.

**Her:** Why do you say that?

**You:** To me, you I sense you are someone really special.

**Her:** What makes you say that?

**You:** Your overall vibe.

**Her:** Well, that would be good. I can't right now, I have to run home.

**You:** Can I have your number?

**Her:** Sure.

*<Make the phone number exchange, and pay her bill at the convenience store.>*

## NOTES AND OBSERVATIONS

The world is a tough place, and not everyone is doing well. Every man is different, but many don't care what the lady does for a living or what her situation is right now. She could be a diamond in the rough. You don't know if you don't try.

Do you remember what we talked about in Part 1 of this book? I made a huge deal about my philosophy about men taking the lead and working hard on their goals every single day. The reason why they do that is to be able to provide for and support the people they care about (family, wives, and close friends). In this example, yes, you were using a "please don't eat that garbage because I will take you someplace better" opener with a lady you are trying to meet. But speaking of upgrades, *you* are the type of person who is himself an upgrade for people in his life. And the way you stack wins every day towards your goals makes you a better man – day after day. Ladies and everyone else around you are going to see that progress in you. That continuous improvement leads to confidence and prosperity, which leads to you knowing at your core you are right for most women out there. The question is: are they right for you.

## IN-PERSON | CONVERSATION 45

**SITUATION:** You have tried asking out a lady who like in your neighborhood, but she has flatly but politely turned you down twice over a three-week time span.

**You:** *<you see her again, but will limit yourself to nothing but a "hi" without slowing down>*

**Her:** Hey! Hi! How are you doing *<your first name>*

**You:** *<smile, in spite of the fact you are surprised at two things right now. The first is she remembers your name and the second is she initiated contact with a new energy of her own>* Hi Charlotte! How are you?

**Her:** *<she is quite talkative, and this feels like the first two interactions never happened>*

**You:** *<wondering if she has changed her mind>* Where were you headed today? Do you want go for a walk?

**Her:** Sure!

## NOTES AND OBSERVATIONS

Per Rule 6 from our Ten Rules, we do not harass women or do anything that can be remotely considered harassment. She has turned you down on two occasions already. Ordinarily, I would recommend not asking her again since they might feel like pestering, or worse yet, harassment. Therefore, you have no plans to ask her out again.

However, sometimes the lady changes her mind and starts treating you entirely differently. Maybe she regrets saying no before. Maybe her circumstances have changed. If you are still interested, proceed. Basically, the point here is you need to adhere to our rules about taking no for an answer and not harassing women by flirting with them over and over when they aren't receptive to it. But she can throw you a curveball later if she changes her mind about her interest in you. A situation that was once ice cold and not a possibility is now a vibrant opportunity. Life has its twists and turns sometimes.

## IN-PERSON | CONVERSATION 46

**SITUATION:** It's the second time you have ran into the same interesting person randomly out in public.

**You:** Hi! If I said "hi, veggie doughnut lady" to you, would that make any sense at all?
*<Background: You haven't gone crazy in this example. What happened is that a couple weeks prior to this you were in a whole foods market and talked to her about doughnuts in the bakery section of the store. She tried to tell you that vegan doughnuts are good now, despite their being like eating hockey pucks before. You were interested, but couldn't close back then. Today you run into her downtown.>*

**Her:** *<she looks over, thinks for a moment, then bursts out laughing at the absurdity of what you just said>*
Yes! I remember you!

**You:** Oh, thank goodness. Otherwise, what I said would have been nuts!

**Her:** *<laughs>*

**You:** How are you doing?

**Her:** *<This time she is in a far more talkative state. She updates you on pretty much her activities over the past couple weeks. Here again, you look for hooks in what she is*

*saying, meaning things you can ask her more about, thereby extending the conversation in a natural way, and learn more about her in the process. If you are feeling possible chemistry and no Ten Rule issues are apparent after all of that, attempt a second close.>*

**NOTES AND OBSERVATIONS**

Your first attempt at an approach didn't work out, but the second one did. That is one reason why you never end any interaction with a lady badly. And you also end those interactions in a positive way because you don't know what might happen next. You might see her again, and things might turn out differently.

## IN-PERSON | CONVERSATION 47

**SITUATION:** You are sitting in a coffee shop getting some work done. You selected a table close to the most interesting ladies in the shop because that makes your work environment that much better. After a couple minutes, one of the staff yells "large hot chocolate for <your name>".

**You:** *<As you walk by one of the pretty female patrons, you say>* Now everyone in here knows I order a children's drink. *<she looks up smiling, and you continue>* Does that diminish your opinion of me?

**Her:** No, I love hot chocolate.

**You:** *<you return with your drink>* What are you up to?

**Her:** A friend had to no-show, and I had already ordered. You?

**You:** I popped in for a change of scenery to get some work done. Sometimes changing locations helps me focus.

**Her:** I understand completely. I can't get anything done at work! It is one of those open office things. Yuck! I should move my work desk here! *<smiles>*

**You:** Hey, I'm taking up a whole table over there by myself. Would you like to sit together? I'll behave *<smile>*.

**Her:** Yeah, leave your baby drink right here <*laughs*>, I won't take it. Sure! <*laughs*> Come over!
<*there you go*>

**NOTES AND OBSERVATIONS**

Being bold and self-deprecating at the same time worked here. Again, be careful about putting yourself down too much. If you do it a lot, that can suck the energy out of the room, and many people might not want to spend time with you. In this case, you were trying to break the ice with someone you wanted to meet. Now you need to quickly inject positive energy and fun into the ensuing conversation with her and just be yourself as you get to know each other.

## IN-PERSON | CONVERSATION 48

**SITUATION:** You see a model-thin beauty while out. You decide you want to introduce yourself...

**You:** *<smile> <eye contact>* If you are trying to flirt with me, it's working!

**Her:** *<laughs>* Huh? What?

**You:** I just wanted to come over and introduce myself. You are just stunning.

**Her:** Oh my god. Hey! Thanks!

**You:** You look out of place, more like you should be in one of the modeling capitals of the world like Milan or Paris. Whatever it is you are doing, keep doing it.

**Her:** I don't know what that would be. It's been a pretty rotten year so far.

**You:** Oh, I'm sorry. How so?

**Her:** *<she and her family have had some struggles financially, and with illness><she starts tearing up>*

**You:** I didn't mean to upset you. I'm sorry!

**Her:** It's okay.

**You:** You are supposed to get 7 hugs per day, and I think you are running short. Come here! *<you gesture for her to move in>*

**Her:** *<she moves in for a hug>*

**You:** *<you give her a friendly hug, then release> <sensing a change of scenery might help her compose herself, you say>* Hey, let's get out of here and get something to eat maybe, or some coffee. Where can we go?

**Her:** We can do that. There is a good place we can walk to from here. We can just leave our cars if you drove here. *<go for it>*

**NOTES AND OBSERVATIONS**

Just because someone looks like a perfect 10, it doesn't mean they live a fairy tale life. And, as I have said before, no woman is outside of your reach, no matter how tall, short, fat, skinny, or bald you are. If you feel attracted to a lady, and there are no Ten Rules issues involved, be bold and act. If she asks where the 7 hugs thing came from, tell her you think it is probably in the Constitution. If it isn't, it should be.

## IN-PERSON | CONVERSATION 49

**SITUATION:** You are waiting in line to check out at a grocery store. Your time comes, and you step forward...

**Her:** Hi! I am sorry it took so long.

**You:** No, take your time. <*smile*> I was just admiring how cute you look from over here.

**Her:** <*smiles*> Thank you for saying that. When I was 18, I hated when guys when would look at me. After I got older, I like people saying something nice. But it happens less often. I asked my older sister and she says it only gets worse.

**You:** Well, if you ever need a boost, come over and say Hi and I will get you squared away.

**Her:** You have made my day! Thank you!

## NOTES AND OBSERVATIONS

I added this example to make a point about women's confidence as they age. We guys can be some cocky, audacious people at any age. Society doesn't, for lack of a better term, shun men as we age. But some women's confidence plummets as they age. They feel they can no longer compete with a young, fresh twenty-something who society seems to adore and who can get pregnant if you just brush by her.

I also bring this example up because the reactions you get from flirting with 5-10 women per day may vary by their age. Like the lady mentioned to you here, when they are 18-24, they might get frustrated by being hit on by every poorly-mannered and aggressive troglodyte who gets within 10 feet of them. Younger women might have their guards up all the time out of necessity. Later, they may be more receptive to approaches from good men like you.

## IN-PERSON | CONVERSATION 50

**SITUATION:** You are walking down a sidewalk, and just as you pass a woman who was facing away from you, she turns around and you get a glimpse of her face as you pass by. She is the most beautiful woman you have ever seen. Visions of a joyous wedding and your future children flash before your eyes.

**You:** *<stunned, you circle back a few steps toward her>* I'm sorry to disturb you. But I was walking past you a moment ago when you turned around, and you are the most beautiful woman I have ever seen. You have this unbelievable combination of health and beauty going on. You are just stunning, and I felt I needed to tell you so, in case you were unaware.

**Her:** *<her mouth flies open, but she says nothing. She walks straight toward you and gives you a full wraparound hug>* Thank you so much!

**You:** I'd bet you don't need makeup at all. You look, I think the perfect word for it would be, heavenly, as-is.

**Her:** *<she comes in again for warm hug #2>*

**You:** *<you realize you need to stop gushing about her appearance and transition to something else>* I'd love to get to know you, if you are available some time.

**Her:** Sure, we can do that.

**You:** We can grab coffee now?

**Her:** <*takes out her phone*> What's your number? We can get together this evening if you are free?

**You:** Yes. Definitely.

## NOTES AND OBSERVATIONS

A few points here:

About touching, some women will touch you first. Be careful about touching her first until you know what she allows and what her tolerance is. Some people don't want to be touched at all. If you want to touch her as you talk, maybe a light touch on her upper arm. If her body language shows she didn't like that, then don't try again until you are certain she trusts you enough. You might hold her hand if you lead her through a crowd of people in a bar or on the street.

Second thing:

Some women are so beautiful to you that it is hard not to go a little overboard in complimenting them, like in this example. I want to be clear about why I don't want you to put anything about your ideal lady's appearance in the compatibility assessment criteria that I asked you to create in Part 1. In my experience, a woman's appearance isn't vital to your long-term compatibility. Many guys have jumped at that first pretty face, overlooked some red flags, and ended up in marriages where they are completely miserable. That happens because they didn't know what they really needed for long-term happiness and satisfaction when settling down with a woman and considering starting a family. It isn't her face, hair, or figure that really matters. Sure, a woman's beauty is a wonderful thing, but if you skipped over making that compatibility assessment from Part 1, please circle back and do that honestly. Please.

> Third thing:
>
> I wrote this book to put forward a mindset and a structured approach that I believe will benefit men worldwide, by the millions, to avoid that type of problem. If millions more of us are acting better out there, developing ourselves, and acting in very high-quality ways, we will be more effective at finding great ladies for us without leaving a trail of damage, misery, divorce, and broken families behind us. That will improve whole societies - worldwide. That is my small contribution to the world. That is my dream.

## Gentlemanly Exits

Flirting doesn't work every time, far from it. You never know what will happen. You only know that your involvement will only leave the lady feeling better off about herself, never worse, no matter what happens.

Yet, sometimes you need to end a conversation, a date, or a relationship. Our Ten Rules still apply in all of those cases, especially Rule 4. No matter how things go on a first approach or in the dating process, don't leave a trail of bad feelings or negativity behind you.

If something went wrong because of your own actions, gentlemen don't leave a trail of Ten Rule violations behind them. If you made a mistake, please consider making an apology and wishing her the best in the future.

If you need to exit because she rejects you in some form, turn that rejection into a positive and learn from it. Exit on a high note and later diagnose what happened afterward. Was there something wrong with your approach that turned her off? Was it your tone, the timing, or the body language? After that, learn that lesson, make any adjustments you feel are necessary, move on. Another lady will be along soon.

It might be there was nothing wrong at all, and she has a boyfriend, husband, or is simply not interested. Whatever the reason, exit in a graceful and impeccably polite way. Like these:

1. It was very nice to meeting you! Take care!
2. It was great talking to you! See you!
3. Sorry, please excuse me. I need to say Hi to the host.
4. It was a pleasure meeting you. Have a good day!
5. Bring your phone out, and "Sorry, I have to take this call. It was so nice meeting you".
6. I've got to grab a drink or a bite to eat from the hors d'oeuvres table. It was great chatting with you! I'll see you around!

> Rejection can hurt, and no one likes disappointment. What can hurt you more in the long-term is regretting not trying. Not reaching out. Not acting when opportunities are there. Not taking a chance on approaching someone could eventually turn out to be a great lady, wife, and mother to your children. Be bold.

EDUCATION
CAREER
INTIMACY
RELATIONSHIPS
GIVING
BACK
YOU
STARTING A FAMILY
BUSINESS
GOALS

# PART 1

# Part 3.
# MEETING ONLINE

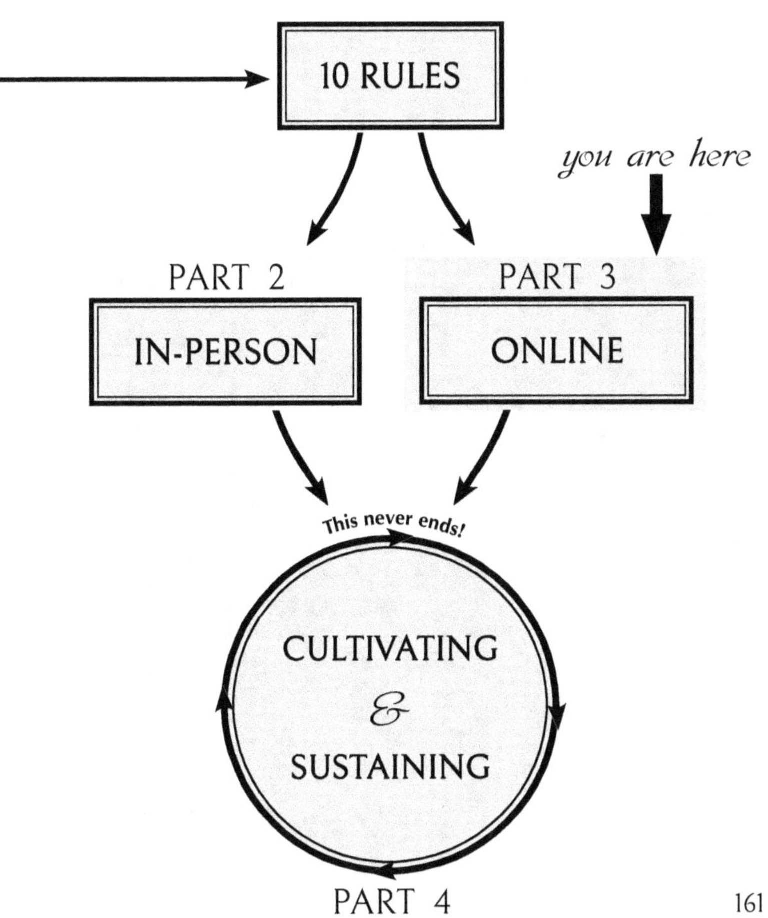

> "Never let the fear of striking out keep you from playing the game." —Babe Ruth

In this chapter, we will cover how to use the various online dating systems and technologies out there to meet great ladies in the same high-quality manner with which we do everything in life.

Everything you need to know about effective online dating will be covered here in Part 3. Specifically, we are going to cover:

1. What is the online dating world? What are the various components and options?
2. Creating a great profile for the various websites and services.
3. Being able to function, stand out, and thrive in online social spaces.
4. Being able to close online and move your interaction to the physical world. By that, I mean moving from sitting at a keyboard to your first in-person date.

## What is Online Dating?

Online dating consists mostly of dedicated websites and mobile apps intended to help people connect for romantic purposes and to find partners for relationships. These services can either be subscription-based or free (supported by ads). There are dozens of dating website and mobile app options.

Online dating should be great, a wonderful and life-changing tool to filter through a sea of possibilities quickly and efficiently. However, it isn't working out that way for many men or women. Too many people report terrible experiences with online dating—for a variety of reasons. This is a problem you will need to navigate successfully if you want to use online technology in your search.

The paid online dating services tend to better filter out the amount of riffraff, fake accounts, and scammers you will encounter, but even the paid options aren't problem-free. They all have problems due to human behavior, and the fact that it is online, an environment which doesn't always bring the best behavior and manners out of folks. Try both the free and paid websites and mobile apps to see what works best for you.

To provide a quick summary, here are a few of the good and bad aspects of online dating:

***The Good***

- You often get informative profiles to read through. That is far better than just going by pictures alone. In fact, many ladies create their online dating profiles thoughtfully and thoroughly. Their complete profiles can help with your initial screening process.

  I know some of you will be tempted to play a volume or numbers game and send connection messages to dozens or hundreds of women on each site after looking at the pictures alone. Many men who do that are normally getting near 0% in their response rates. If you adjust your profile to show you in the best possible light and use some of the eye-catching and fun openers from this book, your response rate will improve.

- You can sift through and consider a large volume of women in a shorter period of time.
- Online dating provides an initial buffer of safety for you too, not just for her.

***The Bad***

- Ladies get bombarded with messages online. The more attractive ladies' mailboxes are always inundated. It is harder ladies to see a genuine message from a quality guy like you. Normally, you must reach out online with something better than "Hey" or "Hi" to catch her eye, and your profile should be appealing.
- Women generally won't reach out to you online. There will be exceptions here and there if you have taken the time to create an appealing profile with great pictures.
- There are serious problems online with toxic behavior from both men and women at all stages of the process, and those negative experiences can turn people off from using online dating services.
- On every platform, there are scammers and fake profiles which you need to avoid.

## Using Texting, Online Messaging, and Email Effectively

I'll say up front that I don't prefer texting or messaging, especially early in the process of meeting and getting to know someone. As communication methods, these aren't as rich as speaking in person or on the phone, even when you are a good communicator and can effectively use emojis. In some cases, you may have a very limited number of characters you can type per message. However, these messaging methods are all very commonplace now, especially when coordinating meeting times for dates or staying in touch.

Since they are so commonplace, you'll need to be able to use these tools effectively. Here are a few pointers:

- ✓ Always maintain a positive and playful tone.
- ✓ Be careful with dark humor, sarcasm, and complaining.
- ✓ If you've only recently initially met, remind her who you are in case she has forgotten.
- ✓ If she doesn't reply after two or three messages, stop sending. Maybe it just isn't the right time for her, or she isn't "feeling it" right now. Maybe she is simply too busy to socialize right now.
- ✓ NEVER ask for a nude or sexy picture. NEVER send one, either.
- ✓ Spell things correctly. Use good grammar. Don't use obscure slang or abbreviations.

✓ Use emojis. I used to think these were solely for children and teenagers, but I was wrong. If you are using a text-based communication mechanism, emojis can help you convey some emotion and sentiment. You can add a smiling, winking, or laughing face in appropriate spots to help avoid misunderstandings.

> Remember, human communication consists of somewhere around 90% tonality and body language, leaving a maximum of 10% for the actual words spoken. When you are using a text-only communication mechanism, the 90% part isn't available to you, leaving you at a considerable disadvantage.

## Dating Profile Creation Excellence

One of the best aspects of online dating websites is that you don't have to worry about mustering as much courage as you do when initially approaching a woman in person. Online also means that she gets to see you presented at your best in your profile, since you've created that beforehand, and it is polished, well-crafted, and honest.

✓ Post multiple photos following our photo guidelines, if the platform allows it, each showing you in a different but positive light. You should post multiple recent photos to avoid looking like a fake or suspicious profile.

✓ Appear alone in your profile photos—with no other people, cars, expensive possessions, or other props that distract her attention or make some sort of statement. Children and pets are okay, if you want to highlight that you have them as part of your screening. Sports activities, hobbies, and leisure activities that highlight your personality are good profile source material. Don't wear sunglasses. Let her see your eyes.

✓ Smile naturally in your profile photos. If you aren't comfortable showing your teeth, then keep your lips together and go for it! It works just as well. Smile with your whole face, including your eyes. Show your whole face, from as many angles as you see fit. Show your whole body in some photos if you feel comfortable doing so.

✓ Wear clean clothes that fit you well in your profile pictures.

✓ Make your profile description clear about what you are looking for. Your profile can do some pre-screening for you while at the same time doing a great job of helping you market yourself.

✓ Consider your personal safety when creating your profile. Maybe only use your first name or a nickname. Don't disclose where you work, show yourself in any work uniform, or provide any details about where you live.

✓ When writing your description, be completely honest but not overly wordy. Good men are in high demand on dating websites. Online dating sites are seen by many women as full of pickup artists, cheaters, creeps, and scammers. If your profile comes across as well-intentioned and honest, and if you use the methods in this book, a good prospect like you will not be on the market long on these dating sites.

I recommend that your profile at least contain:

- a short attention-grabbing opening,
- some bio information about you, and
- a short description of what you are looking for

Like this:

<YOUR FIRSTNAME>

I am what you are looking for.

I am a driven business owner and entrepreneur who is now wanting to settle down. I am a deeply caring person and would very much like to start a family if possible. I am financially stable and don't smoke, drink, or do drugs. I like <hobby>, <hobby>, <music>, <music>, <sport>, and <sport>, and I am a noted grilled cheese sandwich chef and connoisseur.

I am looking for a quality lady with depth of character. I prefer someone who is <ITEM1_FROM_ASSESSMENT> and <ITEM7_FROM_ASSESSMENT>, who loves <ITEM2_FROM_ASSESSMENT>, <ITEM4_FROM_ASSESSMENT>, and <ITEM5_FROM_ASSESSMENT>, and who wants <ITEM8_FROM_ASSESSMENT>, <ITEM11_FROM_ASSESSMENT>, and <ITEM9_FROM_ASSESSMENT>.

A strong eye-catcher like *"I am what you are looking for"* from the profile template above is great. It is great because it is creative, has high energy, and makes her want to ask questions. Alternatively, you might consider one of the other many strong openers throughout this book if one of those resonates with you and better fits your style.

The second part of that profile template is biographical. Insert enough information there so that she gets a good idea of who you are, but not too much. Please be conscious of what you are sharing which might give away your identity or location to people who shouldn't have this information.

The third part is constructed from your compatibility assessment criteria from Part 1. I think you should include some, but not all, of those items in your profile. I recommend being thoughtful and thorough in this part of your profile so that at least some pre-screening can happen on the ladies' side without your involvement. If she sees she isn't a match, then there is no need to respond. Anything from your compatibility assessment criteria that is too personal or private, or which might sound heavy at this early stage should be left out of your profile. You can cover those points in conversations later in the process, when the time feels right.

## Getting to that First Date

Your primary goal in these dating sites or apps is to get to an in-person meeting, phone call, or video chat. The purpose of the phone call or video chat is, if you feel it is worthwhile and there might be chemistry between you, to work toward a real-world meeting. You want to meet in person to start to get to know her better in a more natural, human way. Once you are reasonably convinced that she might be a match for you, then start moving toward the close (i.e., an in-person date or meeting). She might push back, or she might quickly agree.

The location of your first in-person meeting should be a place where she feels completely safe and comfortable. Also try to select a place that is quiet enough for you two to talk.

When making plans, choose something she can look forward to, not just a boring activity. What's better, "dinner" or "that new place that serves seafood by the steaming, spicy, tasty metal bucket full?" Maybe find some events in town that are free or inexpensive. Always keep track of events and festivals in your area, and have them ready to offer as date options.

Never spend a lot of money on the first date. Offer free or cheap date options first. Don't buy expensive tickets for anything, and no expensive meals or drinks. That can come later. Start slowly, and don't do more until she has shown herself trustworthy and worthy of your investment.

Know that one downside of online dating is that some women might be slightly more prone to flaking (e.g., not showing up for dates), since you may not have connected very well yet. Other possible reasons for her flaking might include: she wasn't really interested or serious in the first place, she is concerned about her safety, or she is concerned about how well an in-person meeting might go. Don't be frustrated if this happens, women that flake on you without an excuse or apology are easily replaced. If this happens, simply move on to the next great lady.

### Standing Out Online

Obviously, before you get to the first date or meeting, you need to make a connection with her. You need to stand out enough to get her attention. She needs to see you as interesting, fun, safe, and worth making the effort to explore if you are what she is looking for.

We are going to do dive in to that now, starting with some complete and annotated examples. Everything we do is in accordance with our Ten Rules, so let's quickly recap those before proceeding.

1. Be confident.
2. Have a plan. Always have something to say.
3. She needs to feel safe, comfortable, and unthreatened at all times.
4. Every interaction must be a positive experience for her throughout.
5. Don't be creepy.
6. Don't harass.
7. Never at your workplace or place of business.
8. Pre-screen and assess the situation and environment.
9. Smile and make eye contact.
10. Listen to her. Watch her body language.

The 10 Rules do not change. The *context* of how you apply them is different online. For example, you can only watch for body language cues in online situations in something like a video chat.

> Please use good spelling, grammar, and punctuation in your online communications. Your communications don't need to be polished literary masterpieces, but you don't want her questioning your intelligence due to every message from you being an inscrutable, typo-laden mess.

### Putting It all Together

Let's begin by showing you several high-quality examples of how fast you can transition from the dating platform to either a phone or video call, or meeting her in person. The top portion of each example is the conversation, and the bottom portion has the related commentary.

## ONLINE | CONVERSATION 1

**You:** I imagine you have only dreamed about getting a message from such a physical specimen of a man. Think of how good you are going to look on my arm. You deserve it. We should talk!

**Her:** How romantic, let's talk ♡ 🥰

**You:** I'd like to get to know you a bit. Would you be okay with a phone call or Zoom meeting? Or meeting in-person any place you feel the most comfortable?

**Her:** Let's make a call by WhatsApp? Video call. Do you have Instagram?

### NOTES AND OBSERVATIONS

She's sold on just the opener. Her quickly referring you to WhatsApp isn't necessarily a red flag. For privacy and personal safety reasons, not everyone wants to give out their phone number. This, and the next few examples, are intended to show you the speed which you can get from behind the keyboard to a more human interaction with her.

Her question about Instagram might be her confirming your identity and wanting to check you out a bit before continuing. Or she is offering Instagram's video chat as an alternative to talking on WhatsApp. Either option is fine since both have video options.

## ONLINE | CONVERSATION 2

**You:** I can only imagine the feeling of exhilaration you must be feeling to see a message from such a stunningly handsome man. Think of how your stomach will be full of butterflies before our first date – in fact, you'll be covered in butterflies. We should talk!

**Her:** Lol well written tho tbh it sounds like something I'd imagine you copy and paste. No judgement; it may be quite efficient on your end. Am I completely wrong here? Haha

**You:** Let's figure it out. I'd like to get to know you a bit. Would you be okay with a phone or video call? Or meeting in-person any place you feel the most comfortable?

**Her:** Sure! I'd be up for a phone call

**You:** What days and times work best for you?

**Her:** Weekdays actually - are ya free sometime tonight?

### NOTES AND OBSERVATIONS

Her comment about "copy and paste" might have been because that rather long greeting has a typo-free high polish on it, and that might not be what she is accustomed to seeing in her inbox. That is by design; you aren't the typical guy. There's no need to explain your attention-getting opener, so we get straight to the point of why we contacted her. I think live phone calls are OK (not texting or exchanging voice mails at this critical early stage). You both can get a good sense of what each other is like before meeting in person.

## ONLINE | CONVERSATION 3

**You:** Before you hit reply, I should warn you that I am charming and charismatic at levels science has yet to explain.

**Her:** Haha but that's perfectly fine with me. Before you hit reply I should warn you that I'm one of a kind and stand out from the human population. I'm a diamond in the rough.

**You:** I'd like to get to know you a bit. Would you be okay with a phone call or video meeting? Or meeting in-person any place you feel the most comfortable?

**Her:** Hey! I'm sorry but I really don't use this site much. You can either.... Text me or call me: my number is 555-555-5555 Thanks!

### NOTES AND OBSERVATIONS

Sometimes you will find she matches your own high energy and coolness levels. I love that! That is a great sign. Even from this short exchange, you have hooks to use to transition into a good discussion with her on the call. You can use her mentions of being "one of a kind" and a "diamond in the rough" to get the conversation going when you speak next.

## ONLINE | CONVERSATION 4

**You:** I am the one you've been looking for. Let's talk.

**Her:** I don't quite know how to respond to that lol

**You:** I'd like to get to know you a bit. Would you be okay with a phone call or Zoom/IG/WhatsApp meeting? Or meeting in-person any place you feel the most comfortable?

**Her:** Zoom sounds good.

**You:** What days work best for you?

**Her:** I can do Thurs evening

### NOTES AND OBSERVATIONS

Don't read anything negative into her "I don't quite know how to respond to that lol". Take the lead and nicely get to the point. All you did here again is have a crisp, honest and appealing profile, and a bold opener. Here again, getting away from behind the keyboard doesn't need to be a huge production, it can happen in a flash.

## ONLINE | CONVERSATION 5

**You:** I understand it can be jarring getting a message from a guy with so much sex appeal. I hope you didn't crack your screen in all the excitement. I think you're cute. We should talk.

**Her:** 😆 not very humble of you 😆 But don't worry I didn't crack my screen, I just almost dropped the phone 😁 If you read my profile you would know that sex appeal doesn't excite me. 😉

**You:** I'd like to get to know you a bit. Would you be okay with a phone call or Zoom meeting? Or meeting in-person any place you feel the most comfortable?

**Her:** Zoom meeting feels so corporate 😂 but i would be very okay with meeting in person. Also phone calls. :)

**You:** What days and times work best for you?

**Her:** Any time and any day mostly. What day is best for you?

### NOTES AND OBSERVATIONS

The mention of a Zoom call almost lost her. You powered past that. I suggest you offer her a range of options like we do in most of your examples: video, phone, or in person.

## ONLINE | CONVERSATION 6

**You:** You should listen to that inner voice of yours while you are looking at my profile. She is right--It will be amazing to go out with me. Just think about how good you will look on my arm when we go out! Let's talk!

**Her:** Best pick up line of the year!!! 😂👏

**You:** I'd like to get to know you a bit. Would you be okay with a phone or video call? Or meeting in-person any place you feel the most comfortable?

**Her:** Lol sure

**You:** What days work best for you?

### NOTES AND OBSERVATIONS

***** Alert *** Alert *** Alert *****

Like you have seen in these first few short examples, when the in-person meeting is offered, it is phrased as "Or meeting in-person any place you feel the most comfortable". Use this wording, or something similar, to show her you are safe to meet in all ways. The phrasing in these examples clearly shows that you know she needs to feel safe at any early in-person meetings. Note that we also offer the phone and video call alternatives in the same message. **If you jump straight to asking her to meet in person immediately with no other options offered, she might think you are wanting or expecting sex (i.e. to hook up) even when you have the most honest and honorable intentions.** Always keep what she might be thinking in mind throughout the entire process, and she is definitely thinking about her personal safety.

## ONLINE | CONVERSATION 7

**You:** People are saying that I am the best candidate on this platform right now. I might be the greatest guy of all time. We should talk!

**Her:** I guess why not after all you are the greatest guy of all time
How are you?

**You:** I'm always good. I'd like to get to know you a bit. Would you be okay with a phone call or Zoom meeting? Or meeting in-person any place you feel the most comfortable?

**Her:** Let's meet in person for coffee or lunch if that works for you

**You:** Yes. What days work best for you?

**Her:** Ok cool. I'm free Wednesday or Friday

### NOTES AND OBSERVATIONS

Sometimes she takes charge of deciding the first date. Roll with her suggestion if it sounds good to you.

Also, when answering questions like "How are you?", up the energy in those as a matter of habit in all of your conversations. Don't say "good" or "fine", be "doing great" or something that is better than the standard humdrum answer your hear every day from lower-energy people.

## ONLINE | CONVERSATION 8

**You:** Your instincts about me are right. I would make the ultimate boyfriend. You deserve it. We should talk!

**Her:** Yes, of course we should talk

**You:** I'd like to get to know you a bit. Would you be okay with a phone or video call? Or meeting in-person any place you feel the most comfortable?

**Her:** Are you on Instagram or fb messenger?

### NOTES AND OBSERVATIONS

Instagram video chat or Facebook Messenger would work as well, and are options that many people consider more safe than giving out there phone number. I hesitated to list the various video call options in existence because they change frequently, and the range of options varies by country in some cases. You need to be wary of scams, but be aware that it is normal now to use Facebook, Instagram, WhatsApp and several other options instead of giving out your phone number. If things go wrong, the other party doesn't have your number and these services have easy ways to block unwanted callers.

## ONLINE | CONVERSATION 9

**You:** Hi Pretty! How are you? As you contemplate whether to reply, I should inform you that science has not yet explained why my wraparound hugs and giving me smooches is so beneficial for lowering stress and anxiety and improving overall wellness.

**Her:** Awwwwww heheh 😘

**You:** I'd like to get to know you a bit. Would you be okay with a phone or video call? Or meeting in-person any place you feel the most comfortable?

**Her:** I'm okay with whatever

**You:** Lets figure out something for in-person. What day(s) and times work best for you?

**Her:** Mid to Later this week? What about you?

**You:** Next weekend?

**Her:** Sure!!!

**You:** I'll check in with you when we are closer to then.

**Her:** Sounds good :)

## NOTES AND OBSERVATIONS

Some ladies are confident enough to agree meet in person if your profile and approach are genuine. She sounds serious, and thinks you might be right for her. She sounds willing to take a chance on meeting in person to find out for sure. Her instincts are right - you are the real deal. She agrees to talk more because she is hopeful you are a match for what she is looking for, and wants invest some time to see if she is right about you.

## ONLINE | CONVERSATION 10

**You:** I am the one you've been looking for. Let's talk.

**Her:** How so? 😉 Plz explain.

**You:** I know that I meet any criteria that you have in mind. I know that I will easily pass any screening that you, your family, or most protective friends have. And I know that I will stand the test of time, quality-wise.

**Her:** I see. Good to know 😉

**You:** I'd like to get to know you a bit. Would you be okay with a phone call or Zoom meeting? Or meeting in-person any place you feel the most comfortable?

**Her:** Sounds good, how about tomorrow during day time? We could meet up in _______.

## NOTES AND OBSERVATIONS

If she pushes back or questions your bold opener, coming back with a genuine answer from your heart doesn't need to be volumes or take days to explain over text messaging. I prefer using as few words as possible, blowing her out of her chair with an energy and confidence she has never seen before. You aren't just blurting out pick up lines here, you back it up. The strong opening line was just to get her attention and get the two of you talking so that she can see the real you. These quick in person meetings are more common through proximity dating apps like Tinder, but can happen anywhere. Remember, look for something free or cheap to do for that first meeting. No expensive tickets or meals initially, right? You will have the option to go on a LOT of quick dates in the coming weeks and months, so you might run up a big bill in the process. If you want to keep your costs down, you can just grab coffee, meet in the park, or go for a walk in the area.

## ONLINE | CONVERSATION 11

**SITUATION:** Her profile jokingly(?) mentions the successful guy must get approval from her Dad to date her.

**You:** Hi Pretty! How are you? I feel that you are the type of woman who can see me as more than the dreamy hunk you see in my profile. More than just a tender chunk of juicy man-meat. Let's talk!

**Her:** I am good hbu?

**You:** I'm doing great! I'd like to get to know you a bit. Would you be okay with a phone call or Zoom meeting? Or meeting in-person any place you feel the most comfortable? (Bring your Mom and Dad and most protective friend. I'll pass any tests or screening they have).

**Her:** We can do a phone call 📲

### NOTES AND OBSERVATIONS

Showing that you read her profile helps and makes you stand out as someone who isn't just looking at the pictures. (Reality check: Most guys look at the pictures first. It isn't just you.). Showing your confidence at the same time makes her want to meet you, because no one else would look forward to meeting her closest protectors/screeners/advisors. You do, because if you use the mindset and philosophy in Parts 1 and 4 of this book, it means you know you will pass any tests that she, her family, or friends use to screen guys trying to date their beloved daughter/sister/friend.

## ONLINE | CONVERSATION 12

**You:** Science has not yet explained why women find me so irresistible. I thought I should confide that to you before you replied back.

**Her:** Lol

**You:** We should probably start planning how we can meet, if you think my man-magic isn't too powerful for you.

**Her:** Dm me on insta hehe @accountname

### NOTES AND OBSERVATIONS

Like I say elsewhere in the book, I don't prefer text-based communications. I want to hear the tonality in her voice, and ideally, see her body language in person or on video. Also, when she is taking you to another platform, check the account before you agree to or do anything. Sometimes this can be a scam of some sort, for example, where you might eventually be asked for money. On the other hand, it could be possible she simply prefers starting with DMs (direct messages) in Instagram.

## ONLINE | CONVERSATION 13

**You:** You know that deep sigh of relief that you have been imagining yourself one day releasing when you've met the real deal? Can you picture the tension and disappointment finally wafting away and being replaced with hope and happiness? Let's talk.

**Her:** Hey! I was picturing as I read through your message

You should add me on Instagram! Let's chat there. Add me: accountname 😂

I like you already

**You:** I'd like to get to know you a bit. Would you be okay with a phone call or Zoom meeting? Or meeting in-person any place you feel the most comfortable?

**Her:** Absolutely. We can def meet. Text me my number is 5555555555

### NOTES AND OBSERVATIONS

She sounds slightly hypnotized by your opener. This early offer to connect on Instagram might be a red flag that she isn't serious or real, but you can push a little more by asking for that phone call or meeting. If she comes back with a real number, that is great. You see that used constantly in these examples, and that is the right thing to do because it quickly filters out scammers, catfishers, time-wasters, and other fakes. As a screening technique for us, it is pure gold.

## ONLINE | CONVERSATION 14

**You:** People are saying that I am the best candidate on this platform right now. I might be the greatest guy of all time. We should talk!

**Her:** 😂

Really? They don't say that you seem pretty confident?

I look forward to finding out 😂

**You:** I'd like to get to know you. Would you be okay with a phone or video call? Or meeting in-person any place you feel the most comfortable?

**Her:** I'm comfortable with a phone call for now. Doesn't feel good meeting in person when I barely know someone, but I'm open to it once we've connected and feel there is good chemistry 😊

### NOTES AND OBSERVATIONS

Again, some ladies are only good with limited communication options until the trust is there between you. She has opened the door to a phone call, in this case, don't press her for other options. If a great lady opens the door a little and you are interested in her, go through that door. She will see your quality within the first few minutes of that phone call, and if all goes well from you're your point of view, you can close that call by asking her for that first in-person date.

## ONLINE | CONVERSATION 15

**You:** Whew! Rough day today. I was jogging back from an out-of-state triathlon, and when I was nearly home, I heard a faint "mewww, mewww" at a distance. It was coming from the tiniest little kitten, stranded up a tree. Without a thought for my own safety, I mustered the strength to shinny up the tree—the kitten somehow managed to climb nearly 200 feet up! As I worked my way down, a little girl came by to retrieve her lost kitten. A throng of townspeople gathered and started cheering and chanting my name. I know what you must be thinking, but no, I'm just a man like any other. Just one who smells like tree bark, moss, and kitten right now. Anyway, enough talk about a typical day in my life. I saw your profile and I think you're cute. Let's talk!

**Her:** Hey
So long!!!!!!!!
Lol
Nice to meet you :)

**You:** I needed to stand out in your inbox somehow.
I'd like to get to know you a bit. Would you be okay with a phone or video call? Or meeting in-person any place you feel the most comfortable?

**Her:** Sure we can

**You:** What days work best for you?

**Her:** Any days fine for me. I'm wfh anyways

### NOTES AND OBSERVATIONS

***Warning:*** We both know you want to say "that's what she said" to her "So long!!!!!!!!" reaction. Please resist the temptation. She might think that's crass or a turnoff, at least at this early stage.

A little innocent lie or harmless confession, or two or three, isn't a bad opener. The length of this type of opener will catch her eye in her inbox. Whether she see the humor in your little slightly exaggerated story is a gamble. But it beats "hi" or "hey" by a mile, and that will show in your results.

## ONLINE | CONVERSATION 16

**You:** If you are into bad boys, as you can sense I might be from my photos, I'm your guy. I'll have you know that I don't always wash my hands for the full 20 seconds - sometimes I stop at 17 or 18.

**Her:** Oh man..not a full 20 seconds, I too like to live dangerously. Sometimes, I turn my turn signal off *before* I get all the way into the lane. We're gonna be a regular Bonnie and Clyde

**You:** I'd like to get to know you a bit. Would you be okay with a phone or video call? Or meeting in-person any place you feel the most comfortable?

**Her:** But I could do a phone call (initially) and graduate to video chat if the vibe is right.

Do you have snap? That at least has voice messages we could trade without trading numbers..ya know, in case im a psycho

### NOTES AND OBSERVATIONS

Joking about something bad, like in this example about the 2020-2021 pandemic, can backfire. Snapchat has a video call option as well.

## ONLINE | CONVERSATION 17

**You:** I can only imagine how excited you are as you note this day on your calendar - like a holiday, to mark my glorious arrival in your life! Every year you can celebrate this day and laugh about what you now call the "Pre-Euphoric Period". We should talk!

**Her:** I love the confidence! Hahaha

**You:** I'd like to get to know you a bit. Would you be okay with a phone or video call? Or meeting in-person any place you feel the most comfortable?

**Her:** I think we can start with a phone call first. 😂

**You:** Which days and times are best for you?

### NOTES AND OBSERVATIONS

We might joke a lot in our openers. Don't get distracted by that. The lady can still feel your confidence and energy in *how* you said the opener to her, and what she sees about the real you reflected in your polished profile. All of that stuff matters to present yourself as fun, cool, safe, and interesting.

## ONLINE | CONVERSATION 18

**You:** I can only imagine the feeling of exhilaration you must be feeling to see a message from such a stunningly handsome man. Think of how your stomach will be full of butterflies before our first date -- you'll be covered in butterflies. We should talk!

**Her:** Mhm
Handsome and funny :)

**You:** I'd like to get to know you a bit. Would you be okay with a phone call or video chat? Or meeting in-person any place you feel the most comfortable?

**Her:** Well there is distance between us. I'm in placeA and you're in placeB. We'll meet eventually but you've got to give me the reason.

**You:** I am what you are looking for. And I am likely a major upgrade compared to the other options in your inbox.

**Her:** Lol is that right?
What are you looking for?

**You:** *<can draw from your profile and/or your compatibility assessment criteria. It might be less efficient doing this over chat, so keep gently nudging her to a better venue for conversation>*

**Her:** We can meet

> Where do you live? I live in the "glorious" ______. If not for the ocean, I'd hate it here. Nature is my catharsis. Swimming brings me a lot of joy. Miss the ocean so much during the cold months.

## NOTES AND OBSERVATIONS

*"We'll meet eventually but you've got to give me the reason."* Some ladies need more convincing, and you'll see that often. I strongly believe the "getting to know you" part of the conversation is much better achieved in a more naturally human way. You've got your words and emojis available here. But when you can see and hear each other, you have the richness of conveying meaning using body language, your gestures, your facial expressions, and the tone of your voice. That is why I keep suggesting quickly moving off the dating platform and into the real world if you are both interested. You need to suggest that in a way that makes her feel safe, and without making her worried that you just want sex right away.

## ONLINE | CONVERSATION 19

**You:** I'm what you are looking for. We should talk!

**Her:** Hi! Hope you are having a great weekend. You look really nice:) Do you live in ________?

**You:** Yes, proudly born and raised. I'd like to get to know you a bit. Would you be okay with a phone call or Zoom meeting? Or meeting in-person any place you feel the most comfortable?

**Her:** Thank you for your message. I'm sorry for my late reply. I was in Japan for 3 weeks and needed to catch up with my work.

I've met some people from other app, but I actually have not met anyone from this site yet. I know I'm much older than you..I guess you are just looking for a new friend? You seem really nice and I'd love to talk to you sometime. My # is 555-555-5555. Please text me anytime:)

**You:** I think we can do better than friends, don't you? We can meet and figure that out together.

**Her:** I would definitely say yes if I were younger😭 The last guy I was dating until last year was 31 and we didn't have any issues besides I really wanted to have a family when I find someone I really like next time and he was not ready. It might be too late for me, but I still hope for some miracles! I just wanted to be honest, so I wouldn't waste your time.

**You:** You and I need to meet in person. Let's pick a day that works.

**Her:** Okay. Would you please text me at 555-555-5555?

**NOTES AND OBSERVATIONS**

If she brings up having children like this due to her concerns about her age, and this is going to happen to you if ~35-40 year-olds are in your age range, please do not say anything crude like offering to pump a baby in her right away. In general, I suggest staying away from talking about anything related to having sex in chat with someone you are just meeting. I feel that is something that you two can talk about in person.

## ONLINE | CONVERSATION 20

**You:** I like how you smile with your eyes.

**Her:** Haha thank you ??

**You:** I'd like to get to know you a little. How can we do that in a manner you are comfortable with?

**Her:** Ur a smooth man!! I like that and I would love to keep talking!!

**You:** *<offer a call or in person meeting and go from there>*

### NOTES AND OBSERVATIONS

Creatively complimenting her can work, as in this example. I think most people are fine with being told their eyes are attractive. Avoid dwelling on how pretty she is either in chat or when you two are together. A light compliment is good, but then quickly move to something else. From her point of view, it might be difficult and awkward to saying anything beyond "thank you" after being told she is pretty. What is she supposed to say if you do that over and over? She knows you think she is pretty, move on to something else.

## ONLINE | CONVERSATION 21

**SITUATION:** Her profile says she is a beekeeper

**You:** Hello there! I am fascinated by bees. I would be open to maintaining some, despite being told by a friend that I will certainly not make any money doing so. Your smile, sweet as honey, caught my eye. Anyway, I will stop bumble-ing through my introduction. I await your reply, should you bee so inclined. Otherwise, I will buzz off.

### NOTES AND OBSERVATIONS

Playing off something interesting to you in her profile is another viable option. In this example, she is a beekeeper, and might have heard every bee joke in existence. But she might appreciate the fact that you made the extra effort.

## ONLINE | CONVERSATION 22

**You:** You have pretty eye. I mean eyes. Eyes. (you profile pic appears cropped). Oh, there they are in your other pics. Yep, stunning.

**Her:** Hello! How are you? Hey, thanks :)

**You:** *<Answer her question in a honest and high-energy way, and then try to gently steer her to a call or in person meeting like normal>*

### NOTES AND OBSERVATIONS

Here we take something odd and quickly spin it into the beautiful compliment we intended. Few guys would go down this path, so this twisted yet humorous opener might help you stand out in her inbox. Just don't accidentally insult her in some way.

## ONLINE | CONVERSATION 23

**You:** I understand that I might not be your normal choice appearance-wise, myself being bowling shoe unattractive. You'll like me otherwise. Your being pretty, well frankly that's good for me. Plus, I imagine you are likely interesting. Let's talk it over.

**Her:** You're adorable 😍 what are you talking about?

**You:** I do better in person, or so I think. Let's meet. Please pick a place you are comfortable with, and let's find a day that works. I only ask that it be quiet enough so that I can hear you, and clear your schedule so that we have enough time.

**Her:** I so suck at this site 😐
Would you like my number or something?

**You:** *<agree, and progress toward meeting in person>*

### NOTES AND OBSERVATIONS

There are two points I want to make with this short example.

1) A little light self-deprecating humor is okay, as in this example, in my opinion. Continuously putting yourself down isn't generally good. And certainly don't put her down either, even if that is how you normally joke around with people. The way this opener is phrased suggests extraordinary confidence on your part, and she will pick up on that.

2). The "I imagine you are likely interesting" line here is borderline insulting, but it is phrased that way to give her something else to reply to. If you like this example, expect her to protest that she is interesting, and now she wants to tell you why that is the case. Telling a woman that she is pretty is good. She has been told she is pretty many times before in her life. Telling her you think she is interesting is next-level, and is often a huge and productive conversation starter.

## ONLINE | CONVERSATION 24

**You:** Care to join me in setting a few world records on our first date? I am thinking: 1) Most joy transferred from one person to another. 2) Widest genuine (i.e., not mechanically assisted) smile. 3) Deepest sigh of relief by a woman when she realizes the real deal just showed up finally. And the world record for the most world records set in a single date. Are you up for all of that?

**Her:** Okay okay you have my attention lol

**You:** I'd like to get to know you a bit. Would you be okay with a phone call or Zoom meeting? Or meeting in-person any place you feel the most comfortable?

**Her:** I'd be cool with that maybe we can grab dinner sometime

**You:** *<continue to make arrangements for a call or in-person meeting>*

## NOTES AND OBSERVATIONS

Again, don't hesitate to be bold in a good way. There are lots of ways to grab her attention online that: show you are fun to be around, make you look cool, make her feel you are safe, and show you are interesting. If you are having trouble getting replies online, using the examples here might just do the trick when it comes to getting her attention. There are several stunning openers later grouped together later here in Part 3 for your convenience. Getting her attention is one important step, knowing what to do once you have her attention is another story. We cover all of those follow-on steps in Part 4. The goal of Part 3 (here) is getting you to that first date.

## ONLINE | CONVERSATION 25

**SITUATION:** She is wearing a Willie Nelson-themed shirt in one of her profile pictures.

**You:** Hello there pretty lady! is that a Willie Nelson reference on your shirt?

**Her:** Yes I guess it is!

**You:** I would like to know a little bit more about you. Would you prefer the phone, or here?
*<gambling on the Willie Nelson thing, you see you can have a conversation with just his song titles>*
I'm "Ashamed" it took a while to reply. It will be "Good Times" either way. Let me know "I'm on Pins and Needles". "I'll Stay Around" for your reply, I know "You Have So Much To Do". "Let Me Talk to You".

**Her:** Ha!

**You:** Whew! That took some doing, but I can keep going on in chat (with long gaps in between sends). On the phone I will have to rely on my charm, wits, and charisma.

**Her:** I guess we can talk on the phone :)

**You:** *<proceed to make those arrangements>*

## NOTES AND OBSERVATIONS

I think you deserve an "A" for effort for doing the research to flirt with her using song titles from her favorite artist. That'll be something that stands out in her mind as she weighs whether or not to agree to that first date. Flirting is fun! It is great putting genuine smiles on people's faces and brightening up their day. Thank goodness for Google and Wikipedia!

## ONLINE | CONVERSATION 26

**You:** Hello there! How are you?

**Her:** Hi. I'm doing well. How are you?

**You:** I'm always good. Thanks for asking! Tell me a little more about yourself please.

**Her:** What would you like to know?
I'm blonde, 5'6. DD boobs, muscular legs, my second toe is longer than my other toes.

**You:** oh dear! Now I am all distracted

I was confining myself to a nice, confined box of purity of thought, and one of your items above disrupted that

**Her:** I'm intelligent, a bibliophile, I love music.

**You:** Would you like to skip the call was aiming for, and just skip to meeting in person sometime this weekend?

someplace where you feel comfortable meeting a stranger, and some place suitably well air conditioned?

**Her:** Skip the what?

**You:** the phone call, where I intended to learn more about you. The proposal on the table now is, should you feel ok doing it, switch to in-person.

nothing dirty

frankly, the DD comment above totally messed up my thinking. You and I might need some private time later.

**Her:** hehehehe. That can happen later. Maybe. First we can certainly speak on the phone. I work until 10 Sat & Sun night. I'm not sure what I have going on tomorrow night, I have tentative plans.

**You:** sounds good. Let's find a time to meet, at a place of your choosing, when you have no conflict. Until then, enjoy your outing Saturday night!

**Her:** I work Sat night. And Sun night. I'm off Monday

**You:** I need plenty of time with you, if we are going to invest the time in meeting. It takes me a while to learn enough about someone new.

And I don't want you to feel rushed around work and your other obligations

But I do want a solid block of time, and your attention, when we do meet

**Her:** No, I don't work every weekend. I don't work that late either. Just sometimes. I am off tomorrow.

**You:** Knowing I am safe, I would just invite you to come over late. That way there would be no rush. But... there are rules about meeting strange men...

**Her:** Could you do a weekday evening, or does that not work for you?

**You:** *<complete the arrangement for the date>*

## NOTES AND OBSERVATIONS

I don't recommend starting with such a standard, bland opener. I prefer higher energy right out of the gate. This example shows the lady dramatically upping the energy and spice level of the conversation early. If she does that, just close on the date, in a nice and respectful way as usual. She is already convinced and interested. Her response to your bold "You and I might need some private time later" is further confirmation.

However, mind your personal safety, as always. You might want to meet her in public first for screening purposes before inviting her over.

## ONLINE | CONVERSATION 27

**SITUATION:** She has a thorough profile with some things you find interesting.

**You:** Hello *<user_her_name>*! I would like to know you a little better. Two things specifically, where were you speaking in one of your pics, and what is the nature of your side gig?

**Her:** Hi! The pic was just me doing a reading at a wedding, but I used to do debate as well. My side gig is a granola business, specializing in completely fruit sweetened granola.

**You:** On a scale of 1–10 where 1 is milquetoast and 10 is the late Christopher Hitchens, where do you see yourself on the debating ferocity scale?

**Her:** I was pretty assertive, but not ferocious, so probably a 5.

*<allow for some questions back and forth about profile content>*

**You:** I would like to know a more about you. How can we do that, preferably in an accelerated time frame, and in a way you are comfortable with?

How does your typical week go?

**Her:** I'm impressed with your initiative! Of course—I'm happy to chat more about it live.

**You:** Want to start by grabbing coffee or dinner?

**Her:** I work a 9-5. So my typical week is a mix of work, side hobbies, and fun.

**You:** At the risk of sounding pushy, I would like a non-trivial block of time with you that first time around. All with your permission, of course, and in a place of your choosing. My only other ask, apart from more time than maybe you normally agree to, is the place you pick is quiet enough so that I can hear everything you say.

^^^ all this I ask respectfully.

**Her:** How about we meet at the _______ at ________ this Sunday? It's quiet, and we can chat for a nontrivial amount of time. Maybe 10:30am?

## NOTES AND OBSERVATIONS

In this example, you ask a simple couple questions showing that you have read her profile and are interested. To her you sound educated, well-spoken, sane, and safe. Meeting in a public place helps as well. I don't prefer 5-minute dates. Short duration dates might not allow enough time for you to work in some of your compatibility assessment criteria questions from Part 1. Shamelessly ask for more time, even for that first date. You are a serious guy with good intentions, and you want to learn more about her. That might take some time.

## ONLINE | CONVERSATION 28

**You:** Hi Pretty! I like your long hair. What are you up to?

**Her:** Thanks :)
Just at work . How about you? You look great yourself :)

**You:** Your are kind to say so. I get a dufus vibe from that picture, but it is the best that I have at the moment. I'd like to learn a bit more about you. Want to talk on the phone, or here?

**Her:** 555 555 5555 if you want to text me :)
I work in a call center environment all day till late evenings so I avoid talking on the phone but I like texting and meeting in person haha

**You:** May I ask, what days are you normally off?
*<work toward closing on the first date>*

### NOTES AND OBSERVATIONS

In this example we try a very simple opener from Part 2. Normally if you do something like "Hi Pretty", you need to quickly follow it up with a question or something else to start a conversation. Here she responds well and is open to moving off chat, which is good. Again, please limit the self-deprecating comments like "dufus vibe". Some people get turned off if you keep talking yourself down, so please be mindful of that if it is your habit. It is okay to joke as much as you like, but remember our process from Part 1 is all about building your natural confidence, being positive, and projecting great energy.

## ONLINE | CONVERSATION 29

**SITUATION:** You see a lady you like who also offers a "corny jokes on command" service in her profile.

**You:** Hello there! If I may say, my goodness you have pretty, almost mesmerizing eyes.

**Her:** aww thats very sweet thank you

**You:** I'd like to get to know a little more about you. How can we do that, in a way you are comfortable with?

**Her:** well Id love to talk to you for a little bit, and if we seem like things could work Id love to meet up

if you have questions fire away, im an open book!

**You:** tell me a corny joke first

**Her:** You got it! whats an astronauts favorite key on a keyboard? .... the space bar!

**You:** rimshot!
What is your schedule like?

**Her:** I work all afternoons - am normally home by 7; and then weekends off

**You:** Is your weekend social calendar normally well-booked? If not, do you want it well-booked, or do you prefer a lot of alone time due to your work and other obligations?

**Her:** I'm always down for company, I live alone; during the week I get enough alone time, and my weekend calendar normally involves at least one get together with my best friend if she's free

**You:** I ask this in the nicest possible way, and with the best and most noble of intentions: Where do you see yourself relationship-wise when you reach my age?

**Her:** I'm currently working a graduate degree, so that will be completed and Ill be actually reaching a goal I'll have been working on for the last eight years by that point, Id like to have a family or at least be planning for one; Id like to have someone by my side who wants that too

**You:** Good answer. Don't take this the wrong way, but I walk down the baby stroller aisle in stores now. And I have no baby.

I also look at baby toys in bookstores

maybe, if things work out, you can help me with that one day, for good cause.

obviously, some other stuff would need to come between then and now

**Her:** I completely understand I do that too! I really want a big family; I'm an only child so I would want at least 3 tbh

**You:** let's see, ^^^ that either sounded super sweet, or like sheer lunacy, to you. Which was it, may I ask?

**Her:** super sweet!

**You:** Hmmmm. We need to meet. Find some place you are comfortable with, and we can sort out a day and time to meet.

No rush. Mull it over. But find a way to take a chance and say yes.

**Her:** i mean I'm definitely going to say yes, you seem like someone I should really meet :)

**You:** take your time. We can sort out the details later. Don't feel rushed, despite my pushiness here.

**Her:** that's okay :) I'm glad I've piqued your interest

**You:** *<close on the details of that date>*

## NOTES AND OBSERVATIONS

Here you share a bit more about what you are really looking for. She correctly interprets your level of honesty as genuine, which it is. This level of openness might be necessary with some ladies to demonstrate that you are real, safe, and have good intentions. But I still want you to move to a more human way of communicating when you feel you want to learn more about her. As we said elsewhere, studies show that communications can be as much as 90% body language and tonality, with that remaining 10% being your actual words. This is too important of a conversation to be missing out on that 90% part.

## ONLINE | CONVERSATION 30

**SITUATION:** She's interesting and sounds fun. Her profile mentions her dog has to approve of you.

**You:** Some dismiss me as some sort of nerd, mistakenly judging my photos. But not you. You see a hunk of man-meat. Someone carved out of granite. Your hero. You should reply back.

**Her:** I'm responding strictly for the man meat
Bruh, lol hi
Hi could have worked

**You:** I needed to stand out in your inbox somehow. So, I tried a slight exaggeration of the truth.
... and I am not above cheating by having bacon in my pocket around your dog.

**Her:** HAhahshaha I think that's hysterical and you have such a good sense of humor
I'd clap the cheeks of your personality

**You:** Wanna meet this weekend? There may or may not be cheek clapping.

**Her:** That sounds fun!

**You:** *<sort out the details for the first date>*

## NOTES AND OBSERVATIONS

A light and playful touch on sex-related content can work, but you risk turning some ladies away by doing that. Even if she starts it, like in this example. As a reminder, NEVER ask for or accept nude pictures, and NEVER send ones of your own. She can show you how beautiful her body is in person, when you both agree it is time for that. Some women will just send you a nude picture. Compliment that, but nicely tell her that you want her to instead show you how pretty she is in person.

## ONLINE | CONVERSATION 31

**You:** Hi Pretty! How are you? Please read the following before replying. Warning: Side effects of dating me can include: Involuntary smiling, uncontrolled giggling, increased feelings of wellness, decreased anxiety, and in rare cases delirious happiness.

**Her:** Lol, I'm good, thanks. Yourself?

**You:** I'm very well. I'd like to invest some time in getting to know you. How can we do that, preferably in person?

**Her:** Well chatting would be a good start

**You:** Would a Zoom meeting work?

**Her:** Am I applying for a job? 😝

**You:** No. However, and I mean this in the nicest possible way, this might be an upgrade offer.

**Her:** Oh, you're an upgrade from what I normally get? That's awfully presumptive
😝

**You:** I gotta stand out in your inbox somehow, pretty lady.

**You:** I should tell you one more thing upfront before we proceed: Science has yet to explain why women find me irresistible. I wish I had answers for you, but I don't. You'll just have to roll the dice.

**Her:** Lol. Is that so...jeez, didn't realize you were such trouble 😉

**You:** I am always zero trouble and zero expense to you. But I do ask for your time...

**Her:** Always zero trouble? Well that's no fun

**You:** I'll use my high IQ, my men-tellect if you will, to mastermind some activities to make up for that.

**Her:** Oh my. Well now I'm intrigued...

**You:** *<wrap up setting up the first date>*

## NOTES AND OBSERVATIONS

Sometimes the first approach doesn't work. Sometimes neither does the second or third. The good news is we have plenty of material in this book for you to draw your inspiration from to get her to "yes", like we do in this example. When you meet, please don't keep pouring on the openers and using this tone. She will probably want to jokingly call back to how you handled asking her out, but move on to just being yourself on that first date. She now knows you have this special gear that you can kick in when you need to and are fun and cool. Now that you have her attention, transition to showing her the real you.

## ONLINE | CONVERSATION 32

**You:** Before you hit reply, I should warn you that I am charming and charismatic at levels science has yet to explain.

**Her:** Thanks for the warning, I will try to brace myself:) I should warn you my hilariousness and delightfulness has also been said to be dangerous. How are u?

**You:** I'm very well. I'd like to invest some time in getting to know you. How can we do that, preferably in person?

**Her:** I'd probably want to talk a little more on here before we met, but when we do meet maybe we could meet somewhere outside, maybe coffee?

**You:** How about a Zoom meeting?

**Her:** That could work, I'd want to talk on here a little more before we Zoomed though. What's your favorite dessert?

**You:** Strawberry shortcake I think. Chocolate cake too.

**Her:** Interesting, good choices, I'm a fan of many desserts myself, in particular ice cream and brownies. Any fun weekend plans?

What's your favorite cuisine?

**You:** probably Italian, but I also like a fat, juicy steak once in a while.

You?

**Her:** Italian is always good but my favorite is probably Indian, I love Naan and the curries. I'm also a huge fan of thai. What are some of your favorite movies?

**You:** You need to come out and meet me. Find the best Naan place, and let's pick a day.

**Her:** Why don't we start with a zoom call and go from there?

**You:** okay. What days and time windows work best for you? *<finalize the plans for the video call to move things forward>*

## NOTES AND OBSERVATIONS

In this example, it isn't easy to tell if she just wants to talk endlessly in chat or if she is serious. I bring this example up because I feel that at some point, you should get out of chat and into the real world. If she is a fake account or a real woman who just likes wasting people's time on dating sites without ever meeting, you need to figure that out. So, in this example, after some back and forth, we insist on meeting using: "You need to come out and meet me. Find the best Naan place, and let's pick a day." You don't even like naan. Your time is just too valuable to have it wasted. If she doesn't agree, it might be best to move on.

## ONLINE | CONVERSATION 33

**You:** I understand that I might not be your normal choice appearance-wise, myself being bowling shoe unattractive. You'll like me otherwise. Your being pretty, well frankly that's good for me. Plus, I imagine you are likely interesting. Let's talk it over.

**Her:** Well that's an interesting way to advertise yourself comparing yourself to bowling shoes but i swiped you back because your profile was intriguing and I thought you were damn cute oh and for the record I am interesting certifiably interesting

**You:** I do better in person, or so I think. I'll get it together. Let's meet - you pick the place. All that I ask is that it is quiet enough for us to hear each other.

**Her:** Is there any specific food type that you like or a place you have in mind

**You:** I can eat anywhere. I would prefer that you pick a place that you are comfortable with.

**Her:** Thai food?

**You:** That'll work. What days work best for you?

## NOTES AND OBSERVATIONS

I don't know why implying she may or may not be interesting works so often for online openers, but it does. For online situations, where she doesn't benefit from hearing your tonality and seeing your body language and friendly smile to know it isn't an insult, please be careful not to insult her with how you phrase that. Maybe stick to the wording here. In this example, she likes your opener (well, sort of). But she likes enough of your approach and your profile to agree to meet in person. Be ready to answer why you felt she was interesting when you meet, she is likely to ask.

## ONLINE | CONVERSATION 34

**You:** Hello there! I hope Cupid followed CDC guidance and wiped down his arrow with an approved coronavirus disinfectant before he flicked one your way due to me, causing you to be so smitten with my picture.

**Her:** It is a very cute pic

**You:** I am also charming and charismatic at levels science has yet to explain.

You're going to like it when we meet. How can we go about doing that, in a way you are comfortable with?

**Her:** And very modest I see. 😉

I am fine with meeting for a dog walk (I bring my own dog) by the river or something outdoors to test the waters. If she likes you, we can go from there

**You:** Because I like you, I'll tell you about my two advantages in this particular test: 1) one of my man-powers is that I can communicate telepathically with dogs/cats/babies and 2) I am not above cheating by having bacon in my pocket.

When are you free?

p.s. I'll translate if your dog has anything they want to tell you

**Her:** I am great with pets...babies are my jam. I was a nanny for over a decade for a family. My "sister" used to bring her girls to me just so I could put them to sleep so she could. It is a gift. Cats love me, but I am indifferent about them.

And bacon helps

But bacon makes everything better. It should be it's own food group so I am required to eat it daily

Good thing it is not. Or I would not keep the body I do

**You:** *<close on the date at this point>*

## NOTES AND OBSERVATIONS

Claim psychic powers, be a dog or baby whisperer, do whatever you need to do to stand out. Confessing to being a little morally flexible with the rules to pass her "does my dog like you test" sounds fun.

PRO TIP: Keep the bacon in a sandwich bag if grease will show through your pants. I am just kidding. Or am I? On the date, maybe use your alleged telepathic powers to claim her dog is on your side, and to get to the next date. Do a Mr Spock mind meld with the dog if it is friendly to you. And be yourself!

## ONLINE | CONVERSATION 35

**SITUATION:** Her profile says she lives in a small town with an unusual name. The Wikipedia page for that town includes an odd story involving pickles. You see your opening...

**You:** The Wikipedia page for your town sounds made up. If that was your creation as a hoax, kudos!

**Her:** That's interesting as I have never seen the Wikipedia page for ______. It's funny though because what they say is a "house" is a picture of the old post office.

**You:** The pickle part of the story was your creation?

If I may be so nosey, being the beautiful work of art that you are, is your dating site inbox full of discussions like this one (i.e., wild claims from guys, and talk of Wikipedia and pickles)?

**Her:** Nope not my creation even though it's funny lol. And nope my inbox isn't full of conversations like this lol

**You:** I'd like to get to know you. How would you feel about meeting in person, at a place of your choosing (i.e., near your pickle part of the state).

**Her:** I would have to get to know you a little better before just meeting up.

**You:** Understood. Would you be okay with something like a video chat?

**Her:** Sure

**You:** *<set that up>*

## NOTES AND OBSERVATIONS

Who in the world would open like that? It is a risk, but she has never seen anything like that in her inbox, and it might catch her eye. Just move beyond the joke quickly in the video call. Talk like two human beings and let her see the real you as you try to see if there is any chemistry between you.

## ONLINE | CONVERSATION 36

**You:** I imagine you have only dreamed about getting a message from such a physical specimen of a man. Think of how good you are going to look on my arm. You deserve it. We should talk!

**Her:** Wow that's a very confident (or may I say Audacious statement! 🤣). That's a pretty good picture I have to say.

**You:** I'd like to get to know you a bit. Would you be okay with a phone or video call? Or meeting in-person any place you feel the most comfortable?

**Her:** Sounds like a plan! We have to figure when and where to meet though or we could chat.

**You:** What days work best for you to meet?

**Her:** Definitely the weekend since I may have to work late. I am of the understanding that it may snow this weekend though

**You:** We'll figure out something we can do safely after that. I'm looking forward to meeting you.

**Her:** Me too! Hopefully I can live up to your expectations heh

## NOTES AND OBSERVATIONS

This conversation looks standard compared to prior examples, but I bring it up for how it ended. Specifically, I would be worried about addressing her "Hopefully I can live up to your expectations heh" comment. That looks harmless on the surface, but remember, we have the Ten Rules. Rule 4 says the lady isn't allowed to feel worse about herself after interacting with you. So please be sure to take some time to build her up when you meet. And no matter how it ends (after one date, or after years), if she is sensitive about living up to any imagined standard, please guide her out of feeling that way.

## ONLINE | CONVERSATION 37

**You:** I'm what you are looking for. We should talk!

**Her:** Hi! How do you think you're what I'm looking for? Haha :)

**You:** I know I conduct myself in high-quality ways, and I am likely a major upgrade compared to the other options in your inbox. You'll like me.

**Her:** Admittedly it's a pretty low bar on here you're right. What is one thing I'll like about you? :)

**You:** I'll prove out in-person. You'll know when your sigh of relief comes out.

**Her:** How do I know you're not going to murder me when we meet in person, Mr stranger?

**You:** Agree to a video call first, and follow your instincts.

**Her:** Ok let's do a video call. Also, how do you know I'm what you're looking for? Haha

**You:** Which days and times work best for you?

**Her:** You're very to the point aren't you? Lol

**Her:** Ok if you answer my question, I'll give you days and times. Deal? :)

**You:** To be honest, I have a list of criteria in mind, and people fall anywhere from 0-100% of a match for that. None of those criteria has anything to do with appearance. You'll be able to piece together what I am interested in over time by questions I will ask. None of my questions are creepy or insane - I am the real deal.

**Her:** Ok I can do tomorrow or probably one night next week

Let me know what works for you!

**You:** *<finalize the details and timing for the video call>*

## NOTES AND OBSERVATIONS

It is okay to let her know that you are a guy with a plan, and you are a guy who has already thought through what she is looking for. She pressed for an answer before agreeing to meet, was blown away by what you said, and immediately agreed. You will see following our process impresses many women. They will like how intentional you are about dating her, how respectful you are, and she will like your candor and general vibe.

## ONLINE | CONVERSATION 38

**SITUATION:** Her profile includes some of her screening items including: "... know how to spell and use correct grammar..."

**You:** Hi Pretty! I tipe real nice, and speak goodly.

Just kidding. How are you?

**Her:** Thank goodness. Lol.
I'm ok. Just got up really. Time to get this day over with because tomorrow is finally Friday.

**You:** Any major plans this weekend? I want to learn a bit more about you. How can we best do that, in a way you are comfortable doing?

**Her:** I have some things to do this weekend. But mostly going to relax at the pool.

You can just message me on here.

**You:** I would like to switch to a phone call whenever you feel sufficiently comfortable doing so.

I cannot promise a typo-free experience for you here.

... me wanting to show myself to my best advantage and all.

**Her:** I understand that. I don't give my phone # out right away though. Just had lots of bad experiences with that.

**You:** I suppose I will need to take extra care with my spelling and grammar then, as I work toward said desired phone call. Let's see what boxes I tick for you, from your profile:

1). I am certainly punctual. My main reason for that is I think it is disrespectful to do otherwise.

2). I am drug, smoke, and disease free.

**Her:** Good start

**You:** 3). I like beaches as well. The most exotic ones I have been too are the Red Sea (Saudi Arabia coastal side); the Greek island I thought were ok, but not around Athens; I liked everything around Hawaii; and to be honest, I also like Miami's beaches

^^^ Were my semicolons ok there?

I don't eat seafood at all. Not allergic, just repulsed.

Dealbreaker alert: I like milk and ice cream

5). I am a Scorpio. I am not into astrology at all, but you did mention that.

**You:** I think I get an A+.

What do you think?

**Her:** I guess your semicolons were ok.

I like milk in my cereal and eating ice cream too. I just buy the lactose free versions.

I don't know much about astrology either. That's my co-workers forte. Lol.

**You:** What is my sane/safe guy score so far? Have I hit the phone call-worthy level yet? I do better in actual human interaction, is the reason for my persistence in asking.

**Her:** You're about halfway there.

**You:** ahhhh. My charm and charisma shine through!

Sorry for the delay is replying. One of my garage doors won't close automatically. To my dismay, Youtube videos are informing me that fixing this problem is outside the range of my mechanical abilities.

Hey, you're small. If I put you up on my shoulders, how would you feel about replacing a high-tension spring as our first date? Can you think of a better way for us to connect than a shared challenge?

**You:** after all, you are "I'm up for a challenge", and I aim to please

**Her:** ?? I think I'm ok not replacing a spring. Just get a ladder lol.

**You:** Don't despair, I will come up with another first date idea, once we find a way to progress past this chat stage.

**Her:** Haha well I shall wait with abated breathe

**You:** Just for reference, where am I at on the rating scale. I think I was about halfway there a while back?

**Her:** Haha. You're at about 75% now.

**You:** Great success!!!

I'll come back with more, to get myself over the line.

**Her:** Haha. Good luck! I'm at the pool but the dang clouds are ruining it.

**You:** I know, but you don't, that the in-person meeting between us is a desirable thing. You should grant me a pass on the remaining 25%, and start identifying where you would feel ok meeting.

**Her:** ???? I need a few more details about you.

**You:** So apparently Scorpio and Capricorn are good signs ?????

**Her:** That'll boot you to 90%

**You:** ahhhh. I will soon vault over 100%

I just now saw your questions. I am trying this site just now because it is free, and I believe I can quickly talk my way out of this and into my area of strength - in-person conversation.

**Her:** Gotcha. Seems genuine. One more question before I decide:

What do you look for in a lady?

**You:** *<answer from your assessment criteria with just what you feel comfortable sharing at this early stage>*

**Her:** Makes sense.
Oh. Another question. How many people have you met/talked to through the app?

Oh I can't wait to be a mom. I babysat kids and kept a nursery so I have "the look" down already.

**You:** I am talking with a few. It isn't as hard as I had heard. In my opinion, getting to consider a good volume of nice ladies is pretty much the only strength of spending time here at all.

I imagine you pretty ones get bombarded on sites like this. That's fine by me, because I have confidence that I can talk. And I feel I am the real deal, and something acceptable will likely shake out. I just need to be patient.

I can explain that, and myself, better. Go ahead and pick out some place for us to meet that you feel comfortable with, and let's figure out a time.

**Her:** I have met some decent guys though and will meet the ones that stand out. I'm not looking for a hookup which is what most want.

**You:** I am not complicated at all. But I am direct. You will like it, I think.

**Her:** When did you want to meet me? I'm by no means perfect so don't get your hopes up too high. ??

should mention my available evenings this week are Wednesday and Friday and Saturday. But a lot depends on the time too. And where.

**You:** *<finish making the plans>*

## NOTES AND OBSERVATIONS

If you already have experience with online dating, you know some of these chat conversations can take a while. In this rather long and wordy example, you have to work up to the point where she has enough confidence that you are safe and meet at least some of her wants before she will meet you. Note the attention-getting humor in the opener, mocking part of her profile in a harmless and fun way. Sometimes the lady is reluctant to give out her phone number, and she states why.

You could, if you are set up for it, offer a call through something like WhatsApp or one of the social media platforms that supports video calls instead like what we mentioned in several examples earlier. You don't have to exchange phone numbers for most of those applications. Note also that she wanted to do her full screening in chat, but I suggest you nudge the ladies to a communication method that meets her safety requirements, but is also faster and more efficient.

A chat conversation this long can go on for days or weeks, and it is easy for it to go off the rails or be forgotten. Why take a chance on missing out on a good opportunity? Gently push her to a better communications option. You will be doing both of you a favor.

## ONLINE | CONVERSATION 39

**SITUATION:** You want to use her profile for your opener. She happens to mention grilled cheese sandwiches in there.

**You:** Hi! I would like to get to know you a bit. Can we do that over grilled cheese, at some place of your choosing?

**Her:** Hi. You're welcome to get to know me, but perhaps we could talk here a bit first? Jumping right into having sandwiches together seems a bit cavalier. I mean, grilled cheeses are a big step.

**You:** I am better the closer the method of communication gets to in-person. I show myself to my best advantage in person first, and phone next. Hence my wish to move to those as quickly as the other party permits.

The whole grilled cheese thing was umm, cheesy. An act for which I don't apologize for unreservedly, since that sounded like a good idea to me

**Her:** I was being sardonic about the grilled cheese. It's a thing that I do.

**You:** I like that. It is like 25% of my personality. Brittany, let's find a way to ether meet in-person, or at least speak on the phone. You and I risk a misunderstanding here, I think. Which could be a wasted opportunity for both. Plus, I want to quietly admire how pretty you are while learning about you, which I cannot do effectively here.

You being so pretty is, frankly, quite good for me - especially during a lengthy get-to-know-you session. I get to look at something pleasant while listening carefully.

**Her:** Thank you for the compliments.

Here's the thing - I took an extended break from dating because it was wearing on me and I wanted to focus on other things in my life. So I suppose I'm a little hesitant to jump back in. But I can agree to speaking on the phone a couple times to see if we want to meet in person. How does that sound to you?

**You:** The simple, and probably smart thing for me to say, would be to agree to the call. But given what you just said about your recent experiences, I am mulling another proposal... If your negative, or time-wasting, or futile experiences started just like this...

Let's abort this online chat thing

...arrange for a not-so-random chance meeting in person. You pick the place. I come over and say hello. You'll know it's me because I will use our secret passphrase, which is "grilled cheese". You size me up in a few seconds, and let me sit down or not. If you say no, and I sincerely wish you a good day and walk off.

^^^ that, or if you can think of another radically different approach, to change your luck.

What say you? Take your time. I am no rush.

**Her:** Those experiences weren't so recent. It's actually been about a year. Which is why I agreed to the call, because that's something I haven't tried.

But your suggestion is intriguing.

**You:** Let's try to change our luck. Mull it over, and reply back when you are comfortable trying another path.

I guarantee you I will smile, thank you, and walk off if you don't feel "it" upon my approach. You waste no time that way.

Ponder it for a while, and reply back.

**Her:** I'm going to the ____ tonight for a couple beers. You can come by if you'd like. No worries if you already have plans.

*<the next day>*

**Her:** Since no one approached me at the bar, I'll assume you had plans.

**Her:** You can call me at 555-555-5555 if you feel so inclined.

**You:** gah! Two problems 1) I didn't see your message and 2) I would have asked for someplace quieter, so that I can listen carefully.

**Her:** What is your suggestion?

**You:** You pick a familiar place, where you are comfortable.

I only ask that it is quiet enough for conversation. Set aside enough time to tell me everything about you.

We meet from scratch starting at that point. I make the gentlemanly approach, of course.

You just be yourself, and open.

No need to doll yourself up either. I would prefer to see your everyday look.

**Her:** You seem quite confident that we will "hit it off" or whatever the cool kids say.

_______ in Northside. Monday?

**You:** *<finish arranging the date>*

## NOTES AND OBSERVATIONS

Experts said this couldn't be done. No one believed it was possible to convert a lady who is frustrated with online dating over to an artificially-arranged in-person meeting and getting her to agree the online portion never happened.

This example takes a small detail from her profile that caught your eye and uses it in a couple spots in cute ways. If she sounds like she wanted to not engage but is talking to you, but offering her the in-person meeting might win her over. Don't give up to easily on someone truly interesting. Be creative!

## ONLINE | CONVERSATION 40

**SITUATION:** Sometimes the conversation doesn't go well

**You:** *<You crisply drop a brilliant opener from this book, or of your own creation>*

**Her:** *<Is negative, puts you down, insults you, or is wasting your time>*

### NOTES AND OBSERVATIONS

If the conversation is clearly not going in a positive direction, or she is bitter and nasty to you, just cut bait. Don't say anything negative back, even though you may be insulted or angry. Clapping back in this type of situation would be a violation of Rule 4, which is "Every interaction must be a positive experience for her throughout". It is her fault for going negative here. You should say nothing and move on. Or you can just say something like: "I wish you all the best. Good luck!", and nothing further. We live by our rules and principles, even when others don't. You won't feel better about yourself by replying to her negativity with more negativity. It is a waste of time, and you have 20 more great ladies in line right behind this one to get to, and they all serious women who will treat you better.

## Online Opener Treasure Chest

| I am the one you've been looking for. Let's talk. |
|---|
| You know that deep sigh of relief that you have been imagining yourself one day releasing when you've met the real deal? Can you picture the tension and disappointment finally wafting away and being replaced with hope and happiness? Let's talk. |
| I understand it can be jarring getting a message from a guy with so much sex appeal. I hope you didn't crack your screen in all the excitement. I think you're cute. We should talk. |
| Think of how good you are going to look on my arm. You deserve it. We should talk! |
| Warning: Side effects of dating me can include: Involuntary smiling, uncontrolled giggling, increased feelings of wellness, decreased anxiety, and in rare cases delirious happiness. |
| Hi Pretty! How are you? As you contemplate whether to reply, I should inform you that science has not yet explained why my wraparound hugs and giving me smooches is so beneficial for lowering stress and anxiety and improving overall wellness. |
| You may notice today that, after perusing my profile, birds seem to sing more sweetly. The sun shines more brightly. Food tastes better. Yes, that is the effect I have on women. Do what you know is right and reply back to find out more. |
| People are saying that I am the best candidate on this platform right now. I might be the greatest guy of all time. We should talk! |

| |
|---|
| Care to join me in setting a few world records on our first date? I am thinking: 1). Most joy transferred from one person to another. 2). Widest genuine (i.e., not mechanically assisted) smile. 3). Deepest sigh of relief by a woman when she realizes the real deal just showed up finally. And the world record for the most world records set in a single event. Are you up for all of that? |
| I hesitated to post such a sizzling pic. Being this hot can be a burden. Will women throng to me because they only see steamy man-meat? Not you, I can tell. Let's talk! |
| Many people say the experience of going out with me is the highlight of their year. Some say I am the greatest dating partner of all time. I say this to let you know what you might be in for as you contemplate hitting reply. |
| Some dismiss me as some sort of nerd, mistakenly judging my photos. But not you. You see a hunk of man-meat. Someone carved out of granite. Your hero. You should reply back. |
| Before you hit reply, I should warn you that I am charming and charismatic at levels science has yet to explain. |
| Science has not yet explained why women find me so irresistible. I thought I should confide that to you before you replied back. |
| I understand that I might not be your normal choice appearance-wise, myself being bowling shoe unattractive. You'll like me otherwise. Your being pretty, well frankly that's good for me. Plus I imagine you are likely interesting. Let's talk it over. |

| |
|---|
| We both know you see something special in my profile. You can feel there is far more to that hunky piece of man-meat you see. You're right. And you're in luck... Your superhero is taking applicants for a cute yet plucky sidekick. Let's talk! |
| Think of how good you are going to look on my arm. Imagine how you are going to savor every moment of dating me. We should talk! |
| I hope you are seated. Grab the armrests and steady yourself, because I am about to rock your world with an irresistible opening line. Are you a botanical garden? Because I'm filled with butterflies! How am I doing with the flirting? Let's talk it over. |
| I hope you are seated. Grab the armrests and steady yourself, because I am about to rock your world with an irresistible opening line. Are you a cup of tea? Because you are unbearably hot! How did do? Let's talk it over. |
| Hello there! Just on case you don't know the effect you can have on people, an involuntary whistle came out of my mouth when I saw your picture. I had to take a moment to enjoy how pretty you are. |
| I imagine you have only dreamed about getting a message from such a physical specimen of a man. Think of how good you are going to look on my arm. You deserve it. We should talk! |
| I feel that you are the type of woman who can see me as more than the dreamy hunk you see in my profile. More than just a tender chunk of juicy man-meat. At the same time, think of how good you will look on my arm. Let's talk! |

I should warn you upfront, science cannot explain why women find me so irresistible. Some say I am the best guy in the world. I was voted Discouraged Dating Ladies magazine's <current_year> Hope of the Year. We should talk!

I'm the real deal. Will you be just deliriously happy with me, or feel you should shout that I am the ultimate man from mountaintops, I don't know. Let's talk to find out!

I can only imagine how excited you are as you note this day on your calendar - like a holiday, to mark my glorious arrival in your life! Every year you can celebrate this day and laugh about what you now call the "Pre-Euphoric Period". We should talk!

Before you whack the reply button, take a moment to recover from what must be an enormous adrenaline rush from getting a message from such a hottie. Whew! That's better. We should talk!

I can only imagine the feeling of exhilaration you must be feeling to see a message from such a stunningly handsome man. Think of how your stomach will be full of butterflies before our first date -- you'll be covered in butterflies. We should talk!

You should listen to that inner voice of yours while you are looking at my profile. She is right--It will be amazing to go out with me. Just think about how good you will look on my arm when we go out! Let's talk!

I know what you must be thinking: Who is the studmuffin before me, and why does he have so much game? Let's talk!

| |
|---|
| You have an honest face--like someone I can confide in. Well, here goes... You know those 80 million votes the old guys are arguing about? That was all me. Whew, I feel better! Hey, look up some Youtube videos on giving a hand and wrist massage before our first date. I am still hurting from filling in all those little circles. |
| Before you hit reply, I should warn you that I am charming and charismatic at levels science has yet to explain. |
| Whew! Rough day today. I was hiking back from an out-of-state triathlon, and when I was nearly home, I heard a faint "mewww, mewww" at a distance. It was coming from the tiniest little kitten, stranded up a tree. Without a thought for my own safety, I mustered the strength to shinny up the tree - the kitten somehow managed to climb nearly 200 feet up! As I worked my way down, a little girl came by to retrieve her lost kitten. A throng of townspeople gathered and started chanting my name. I know what you must be thinking, but no, I'm just a man like any other. Just one who smells like tree bark, moss, and kitten right now. Anyway, enough talk about a typical day in my life. I saw your profile and I think you're cute. Let's talk! |
| Your instincts about me are right. I would make the ultimate boyfriend. You deserve it. We should talk! |
| I can read your mind. Your thinking: "Look at that hunk of man-meat! Why have hamburger when I can have steak? And you're right. I am the best guy on here, and probable the greatest guy of all time. So, go ahead and reply back... |

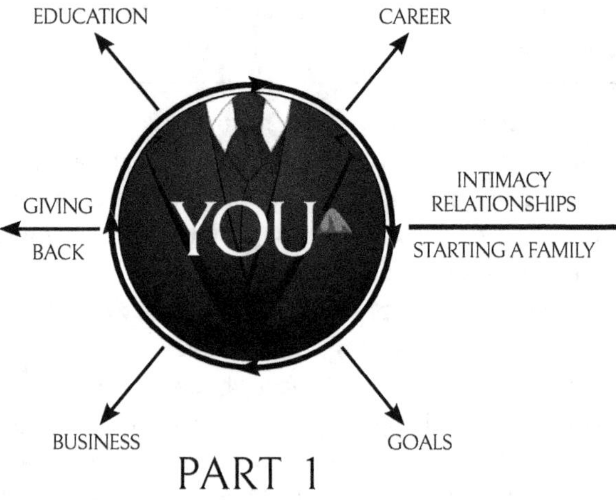
EDUCATION
CAREER
INTIMACY
RELATIONSHIPS
GIVING
BACK
YOU
STARTING A FAMILY
BUSINESS
GOALS

# PART 1

# Part 4.
# CULTIVATING & SUSTAINING

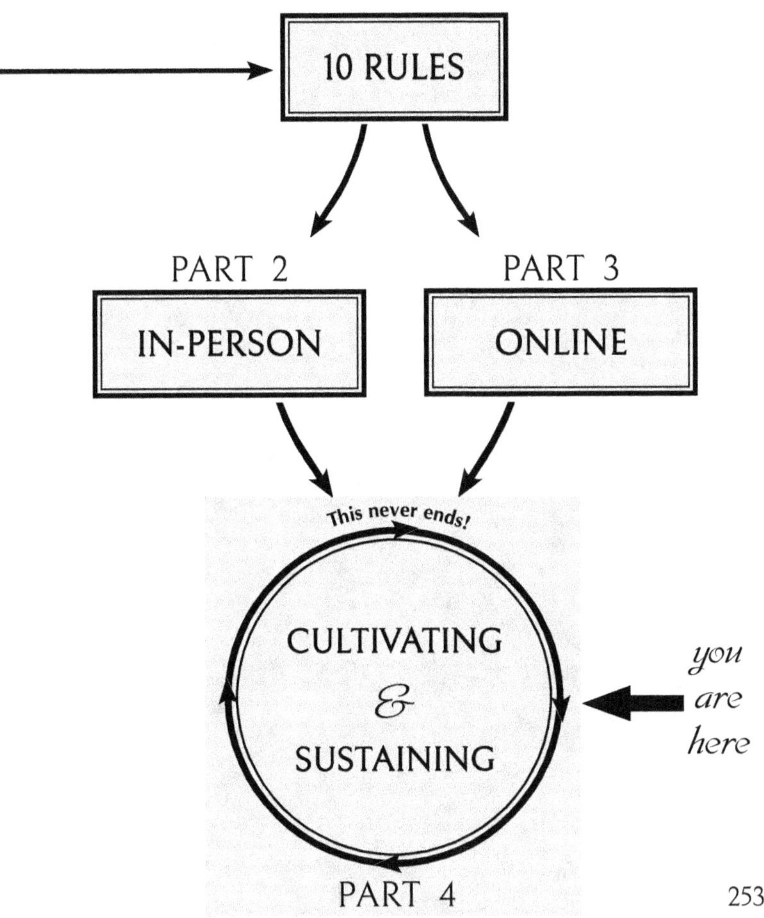

> "Hebban olla vogala nestas hagunnan hinase hic enda thu uuat unbidan uue nu" —Old Dutch, 11th century A.D., author unknown
>
> Translated: "Have all birds begun nests, except me and you—what are we waiting for?"

The quote above was found scribbled in the margins of a Latin manuscript made by a monk in a European monastery a thousand years ago. Spare a thought for the anguished, lonely soul who penned this. Let's not let that ever be you.

## Dating

*Yes, I know she's pretty. Focus! Don't mess this up.*

At this point, you've arranged for a first date using one of the methods from Part 2 or Part 3. From her point of view, she trusts you just enough to meet. She is interested and curious enough to spend time with you. Now what?

You need to use this time to slowly start learning more about her. From your point of view, you need to figure out if you can see yourself being happy with her in the future. Is she really someone you would want in your life for any extended amount of time? You've carefully thought through and methodically identified what you are ideally looking for in a woman in your compatibility assessment criteria from Part 1. While having fun and enjoying the dating process, your goal now is to see how compatible she is with you using your assessment criteria.

From 0% - 100%, what is the right compatibility threshold number for you? What is the pass or fail level, for lack of a better term? That specific threshold value is up to you to decide. I think you need to date at least a few ladies to see what range they all fall in. Those data points should help inform you how hard or soft your assessment might be. Be as hard or soft as you need to be. The stakes, in terms of your personal happiness, couldn't be higher.

Maybe you have some non-negotiable item in your assessment that a particular lady doesn't meet, but she is at 85% otherwise? Maybe another is a 75% match per your assessment, and you don't feel that strongly about the remaining 25%. Ultimately, what I recommend is aiming for 90-100%. 100% is achievable, depending on how high you set the bar in the assessments. What I am begging you to do is not settle for less than you deserve. Don't cave because of a pretty face, you feel too old, or because you have been lonely too long. Don't settle for less than what will put you on a course for long-term happiness.

Don't do what an old expression says and "take her home and learn to love her." Please don't mistake some other feeling for pure love and override or ignore what your compatibility assessment is telling you.

If she is at 100%, do you propose marriage to her on the spot? No, please don't. Give yourself some time to be sure. You know quality in your heart when you see it, but as a reminder, I strongly recommend you track what you are looking for in a logical sense plus what you are seeking in an emotional connection in those compatibility assessment sheets. Including both types of criteria in your compatibility assessment will help you one fine day when you sit down to decide if you really love her or if what you are feeling is something else.

We have some ground to cover before we get to that step.

## Let's Go!

With that higher-level goal in mind, how should you proceed with the dating process? You do that in the same high-quality way that you do everything else in your life.

### *Mindset*

✓ Relax. Have fun. Get her laughing.

✓ Be your best. Be yourself.

✓ Show yourself in a positive light, whether that is displaying healthy ambition, how you constantly learn and grow as a person, or your depth of character. Show that you are on a good path in life and have interesting and productive things going on. Show that you are interested in her as a person.

✓ Always remember your manners: "Thank you," "Yes, sir," and "Yes, ma'am." This shows her how you treat people, whatever their position in life.

✓ Don't let anyone waste your time. If she cancels dates without good reason, "flakes," or makes you wait around too much, move on to someone else. Your time is too valuable.

✓ Don't be too available. As counterintuitive as this might sound, she might think there is something wrong if you are always free to spend time with her (e.g. she might think you have no friends, or are clingy or needy).

***Planning***

- ✓ Be punctual. Always be on time for dates. This shows her that you feel she is important. If you need to cancel or postpone a date for some reason, tell her.
- ✓ Be confident and decisive when setting up dates. By that, I mean make definite plans (e.g., "Let's meet Thursday at <location> for coffee at <time>."). Say with a respectful tone and smile: "Let me get your number," as opposed to asking for it weakly. Never say, "I'll think about it." Don't be wishy-washy, and consciously try to avoid using the words "maybe" or "try" at any point when making plans with her.
- ✓ Clean your vehicle, your home, and anything else she will see.
- ✓ Your clothes don't need to be expensive or flashy, but they do need to be clean and fit you well.
- ✓ Take care of your hygiene and grooming from head to toe. A clean, soapy smell is fine all over. Consider breath mints.
- ✓ Consider stocking your refrigerator with more than just beer, ketchup, and pickles before she visits.
- ✓ Have a list of interesting upcoming local events and date ideas ready.
- ✓ If intimacy is imminent, consider the state of your bed linens and pillows. If your underwear is full of holes, or is mostly just waistbands, consider getting some new ones.

***Conversation***

✓ Smile. Show her you are fun to be around. Get her laughing.

✓ Listen carefully to her, without interrupting her.

✓ Learn her name. Use her name in conversation. Put her information in the contacts in your phone. (Don't be that guy who forgot his date's name.)

✓ Make jokes, but NOT about her in any way. Consider completely avoiding dark or off-color jokes. Even if that is something you like, you don't know her well enough yet to know how an edgy joke will go over.

✓ Slip in a few bits of information about yourself here and there in the conversation. Describe yourself in interesting ways.

✓ Be present, not fiddling around with your phone. Put that thing away and focus on her. She has given you the gift of her time—use it wisely to get to know her. Your phone can wait.

✓ Make eye contact. I said *eye* contact; do not look at her mouth, her breasts, or anywhere else. You can take a brief, respectful glimpse elsewhere when she isn't looking.

✓ Ask questions that are subtle and nuanced. You want to see if she aligns well with your criteria from your compatibility assessment scorecard.

✓ Ask her opinion, then listen with an open mind. Don't turn around and criticize or judge what she says.

✓ Observe how she reacts around children, the elderly, and other people in general.

✓ Read her social cues toward you. Here are a few positive signs:

- She smiles, especially whole-face smiles. She laughs.
- She finds ways to touch you.
- She answers your phone calls and texts quickly (within reason). This shows you are a priority for her.
- She bats her eyelashes.
- She plays with her hair.

✓ Find out what she wants in life and what she is doing.

✓ Laugh at her jokes even if they are not that funny, but don't overdo it.

✓ Don't give short answers to her questions. Try to aim for maybe a couple of sentences, but do not turn your answer into a lengthy monologue. You don't want to ask her too many questions that call for just one-word answers, either.

✓ In conversation, it is fine to refer back to something you two shared earlier, but don't overdo that. Don't repeat yourself or your stories.

✓ Regarding touching, that is a sensitive subject and varies per person. It might be okay to briefly touch her upper arm in conversation. If you are guiding her in a crowded setting, it might be okay to hold her hand lightly, or touch her middle or lower back. If her body language shows she doesn't appreciate any touch, respect that. It might be okay to hug as a greeting and/or on departure, but again follow her cues. Don't touch or hug her in a creepy way, ever, nor in a way that makes her feel unsafe or like she is being felt up.

✓ Have good posture and use open gestures.

✓ Make her feel special.

### Having Something to Say

There are millions of ways the conversion on a date can go, so we obviously cannot cover every possibility here. However, you can draw interesting and productive conversation ideas from the following:

1. Your assessment scorecard for her, taking care to not turn the conversations on your dates into interrogations.
2. Your genuine interest in her as a person, including her happiness and well-being.
3. Your shared values. Your shared interests.
4. Continue to think of and treat her like someone you have known, respected, and cherished for many years. This mindset helps you relax.
5. You can—with a mix of humility, confidence, and pride which doesn't come off as bragging—tell her about your recent wins from your work on continuously improving yourself and progressing toward your goals.
6. Use the conversation enhancement examples later in this section if you get stuck.

## Talking About Yourself

You need to be able to hold up your end of the conversation if she asks you about yourself. However, I need to tell you something first.

### ***What's on* her *mind? What is* she *thinking?***

This next section is a gift from me to humanity. For this, people are going to erect statues of me and name schools after me. I might get a Nobel Prize for this breakthrough in human culture and understanding. Why might I receive those accolades? I am going to help you read her mind.

Just like you have your compatibility assessment scorecard, she has an assessment criteria list for you. Specifically, whether she is conscious of this or not, or willing to tell you:

1. She is trying to picture herself with you in the future, wondering if she will feel happy, satisfied, and secure.
2. She has a threshold of how "together" you are that you must meet. She will only date someone who has himself "together" at least 90%. (The specific number will vary per lady).
3. She wants you to have ambition and be goal-oriented.
4. She wants you to know what you want from a relationship, and she wants you to be able to communicate those wants to her.
5. She wants you to be good at making major decisions but be willing to include her in the decision-making process.

6. She expects you to communicate thoughtfully and respectfully.
7. She wants you to care about the relationship and put effort into it.
8. She wants you to support her ambitions and dreams.

That is largely how she defines a "cool" guy, or whether she is "feeling it" with you. Being a young, good-looking, and fit man might add a few points to your overall score, but this list covers what she wants at her core.

In those first few dates, she knows very little about you. She hopes you will meet some of her criteria, and she would like to find out for sure. That is why she agreed to meet you for the date.

> Using the approaches and methods in this book, you will exceed what she is looking for. Better still, you will be continuously improving beyond that level every day. Knowing this is true about yourself will be a great source of genuine and naturally flowing confidence. You can look her in the eyes and be completely honest with her, since it is a fact you are what she is looking for. Whether she is right for you is the question.

Now that you understand what is on her mind, you should be prepared to answer her questions about yourself. Answer honestly, but be interesting and confident. Avoid single-word answers, but don't ramble, either. Having just a sentence or two in mind, something honest that also shows you in a positive light, should normally be fine.

***Questions she may ask:***

1. When was your last relationship?
2. Why are you still single? (You may want to phrase this in a gentler way if you ever use it, but don't be caught off guard if she comes out and asks you this question in this blunt form.)
3. Were you ever married? If so, what happened?
4. Tell me about yourself.
5. Where are you from?
6. What do you do for a living or career?
7. Do you have children?
8. Do you want children?
9. Do you drink? Use drugs?
10. What do you do outside of your work (hobbies, interests)?
11. Do you, or did you, go to church/synagogue/mosque?
12. Did you attend college? If so, did you graduate?
13. Were you born around here?
14. What is your favorite food?

Should the conversation stall or go off track, consider some of the ideas below. Most of these should be good for first date conversation. However, maybe save some of the heavier ones for later dates.

| CONVERSATION STARTERS AND ENHANCERS |
| --- |
| "I would love to know more about you. What's your story? Tell me a little about yourself." |
| "What are the three most interesting things about you?" |
| "When did you know you wanted to be a <occupation>?" |
| "Tell me something about yourself that people don't know." (This could be a unique experience, and incident, and interest or hobby, anything.) |
| "What would you say is your passion in life? What are you passionate about?" |
| "Tell me more about <anything she brings up, really>." |
| Ask how her day is going. |
| "Where are you from?" |
| "What are you interests; what do you do for fun, outside of work?" Find things you have in common (interests, foods, etc.). |
| "What is the most important life lesson you have learned so far?" |
| "What is your typical week like, or normal day?" |

| "What are you looking for in a guy?" |
|---|
| "If you could visit anywhere in the world, where would that be? If you could live anywhere in the world, where would you choose?" |
| "How do you know our host?" (For parties or social gatherings) |
| What are your thoughts on <topic you find interesting/relevant>? "What do you think?" Ask for her opinion, but don't argue in response. Listen. |
| "What is the story behind that <object, piece of jewelry, or item of clothing>?" |
| "What do you think of <topic, event, person>?" |
| "You obviously have great style, could I trouble you for an opinion on this?" |
| "This place is lovely; have you been here before?" |
| "Why, or why is that?" (Asked nicely and intended to get more detail) |
| Find topics or areas of agreement between the two of you, and then explore those. |
| Be bold. Tell her she is great, and tell her why. |
| Have stories ready (draw from daily wins, or maybe your shared values and interests with her). |
| Have your list of interesting upcoming events and date ideas at the ready. |

***Meeting her friends and family***

She might rely heavily on the opinions and judgment of her family and friends regarding potential boyfriends or partners. Your character, intentions, and preparation will help you pass any test or challenge those folks might present.

There's no need to be nervous about or dread meeting any of her family and friends. In fact, you should be looking forward to it, since it gives you a chance to learn more about her.

Meeting her family and friends is a good thing. Keep that mindset, and be a gentleman at all times, of course. Like everything else in your life, look to harvest the wins from this opportunity. Be observant and take it all in. Observe how they interact, and how they care about her, treat her, and protect her.

Her friends might ask you something like: "What are your intentions with her?" Answer honestly. You think she is great. You find her interesting. You want to get to know her. If things work out, you'll make a good provider, protector, and partner for her. When they are done, tell them you are glad they asked the question and are happy for the chance to meet them.

Consider going heavy on manners with "Yes, ma'am," "Yes, sir," "Pleased to meet you," and "My pleasure," especially with her parents or older relatives and friends.

Leave all of them with the correct impression that you aren't the type of man who will ever let her down. You aren't the type of man who lets his family, children, or friends down. You work hard every day to improve yourself and be in a position to support and protect the people that you care the most about in this world. You mean what you say. If you consistently walk that talk every day, her family and friends will see you not only as a great match for her, but also potentially a valuable asset for themselves. They will be secretly—or sometimes quite openly and vocally—rooting for you and her as a couple.

## Progressing to a Relationship

How do you know if it is time to consider her for a potential relationship? Does she meet enough of your compatibility assessment criteria from Part 1 for you to be happy? Have you decided you two are compatible enough to be happy longer-term (i.e., either as a girlfriend or something more)? Many guys leave women guessing as to what their intentions are and how they feel. If you do that, she won't know where she stands.

Gentlemen don't do that; they are crystal clear. If she feels right for you, tell her how great she is. Tell her that she is beautiful in every way and that you want to take another step and be together.

On the other hand, if after some time, you realize she isn't someone you want to have a relationship with, or have a baby with or marry, then move on—keep looking. Do not string her along. Cut her loose so she can pursue her own happiness. You will both be fine.

## Sustaining a Relationship

While most of the content in this book is aimed at men seeking new romantic interests, much of the material also works with wives and girlfriends for men already in relationships. It is useful for any woman who you want to feel special, valued, and appreciated.

The real world isn't all blue skies and unicorns. You must work to maintain a relationship and keep it fresh and exciting. Healthy and happy relationships at all stages need to be continuously cultivated, sustained, and managed.

Just because you made it this far doesn't mean your work is done. Everything we've talked about concerning genuinely caring about her still applies. Everything we have said about the value of flirting works here too—you still want her to feel special and appreciated, even one, five, 10, or 50 years later. If you decide to get married, never stop flirting with your wife, even after decades of marriage.

Never stop reminding her how special she is, and that she holds a cherished place in your life and in your family.

## Gentlemanly Exits

Let's talk about handling rejection situations during the dating or relationship stages, from both of your perspectives.

1. ***She is "not feeling it." She feels there is no connection. She has screened you out.***

   First, no matter what you do, rejection is going to happen a lot at all stages of the process: the approach, flirting, dating, and relationship. Over time, you will build up a complete immunity to hearing "No," "No thanks," and "I'm not interested," and that is far better for you. Once you reach that point of fearlessness, approaching new ladies becomes second nature and effortless.

Maybe she wants to "friend zone" you? Most women use this as code for "I am not interested in you romantically, or maybe not at all." However, for that rare lady, what's wrong with being friends if she is a truly great person, and she really means it? You'll have to decide who falls into that category.

If you are in the "friend zone" and want to promote yourself beyond that with her, she needs to see you in a different light. The responsibility is on you to kindly and gently tell her exactly how you feel. If that works, great. Otherwise, you need to accept the loss and move on to someone else.

I don't recommend spending time in someone else's nebulous friend zone when you don't want to be there. Time is precious, and there are plenty more ladies out there who want to be with you.

2. ***You don't want to proceed.***
   She doesn't, or no longer continues to, meet your compatibility assessment criteria, or you don't want to continue with her for some other reason. It's good to recognize this and accept it once you know, and then gently, respectfully, and tactfully let her know.

   Importantly, no Rule 4 violations are allowed anywhere else in the process, including when ending a conversation, date, or relationship. There are plenty more ladies out there. Move on without negativity, argument, complaint, or nastiness of any kind, even if she doesn't. Be the bigger person, and don't leave a trail of damage and bad feelings behind you.

## Final Thoughts

If flirting and relationships are easily solved problems in society, as some suggest, then why are so many people disappointed in the dating scene? Why are there so many divorces and unhappy couples?

There are too many good men out there trapped in an unhappy relationship or marriage by money, mindset, or children. Maybe fear of change, or shame and embarrassment, prevent them from trying to address the problems underlying their unhappiness.

My whole purpose in writing this book, maintaining the *Gentlemen's Guide to Flirting* podcast and YouTube channel, and financing everything, isn't to make a lot of money. My purpose is to help millions of men avoid unhappiness and misery in their relationships with women. I want men, by the millions, who want to get married, to choose well. I want men, by the millions, who might currently be unhappy in their marriages or relationships, to get on a path to something better. I want you to be happy.

My experience and research tell me the best solution to these problems is starting with making the man better, in every way, in every aspect of his life. That ongoing, continuous self-improvement process and focus will naturally increase his confidence, and that confidence will attract all types of people to him in all aspects of life. That includes women. This book provides specific guidance on how to go about finding intimacy in relationships when you are ready for that step. That process will work for you, too, but let's briefly look down the road a bit first. I want you to know what might be coming, and to give you some options on how to think about each possibility.

The following tips are distilled wisdom from hundreds of men, tips collected over decades. Some of this is hard to hear, but you might just need to hear it. You're in for some tough love, so strap in.

**TIP 1:** Your happiness, wellness, and satisfaction are crucial. This is non-negotiable. If you think back to Part 1, recall that you and your career, business, education, and goals should also be among your top priorities. This priority arrangement isn't selfish at all. All that effort isn't for you. You work hard to improve yourself to provide for and be the best possible asset to everyone you care about: your family, children, and close friends. However, being a gentleman does not require you to be a pushover or a doormat. Sometimes you need to move forward by removing someone who might be very close to you from your life. Sometimes you need to let go of someone who isn't treating you right and move on—for yourself and for the greater good.

If you find it necessary to cut ties with a lady, know that the techniques you have picked up here will help you attract an abundance of beautiful, high-quality women to choose from—women who will appreciate you and want to be with you, whenever you are ready.

**TIP 2:** Some women will decide to "test" you from time to time to see if you are still the good provider, protector, and mate that she thought you were. These tests can come in a variety of forms, but they generally include some undesirable deviations from her normal behavior toward you. Things might be fine for months, but then, out of the blue, she will pick an argument with you over something that seems small. She might somehow challenge your role as a man or your authority or dignity or somehow insult you. She might find some other ways to be disrespectful to see how you react, or whether you let her get away with it. If you are with a woman who does this and you fail the tests by not handling them in some appropriate way, she might eventually decide you are not worthy of her respect, or not "cool," and the situation can devolve from there over months or years.

Basically, my advice to you is women who test or don't respect you need to understand that they can be replaced with women who will treat you better—and that you can be happier completely alone. Your being unhappy in any relationship is unacceptable. With this book, you have the tools and mindset to find someone better suited for you to be in a relationship with. Don't scream at her and tell her she can be replaced—that is hurtful. Show her calmly that she needs to do better, because you have other options if she doesn't.

If you are already in a relationship and are unhappy, you can try to use some of the techniques in this book to see if she will start to see and treat you differently. Go back through Part 1 and assess what you are doing to continuously improve yourself. Maybe she doesn't think you are meeting her own wants or requirements, or that you have failed one or many of her "Is my guy still cool?" tests over time. Help her see you in a different light. No matter the result, you need to be happy. Life is too short.

**TIP 3:** Let's discuss being "likable" versus being "lovable." We can think of this in the context of unrequited love, or I think a man or a woman can love someone without liking them.

I see this play out often when one party in a relationship is pressuring the other to get married. The party resisting might like their partner, but they don't love them yet. If that never changes, maybe one party isn't being or acting "lovable."

For example, I know a retired US Navy SEAL who has a girlfriend who is pressuring him to get married. You may have heard the phrase, "shit or get off the pot." She has said that to him, word-for-word, trying to force him into marriage. If you ask her why she loves him, she can quickly list a lot of things he does and great character traits he has which make him lovable to her. If you ask him the same question about her, despite him liking how pretty, fit, and funny she is, he says she is controlling and unpleasant in ways that don't meet his personal compatibility assessment criteria for a wife. Even our bravest and most revered military heroes aren't spared this experience, so don't feel bad if I am describing your situation. You aren't alone.

So, should you shit or get off the pot? First, you are a high-quality upgrade for most ladies, so these crude terms don't apply to you. Second, and crucially, does she meet enough of your compatibility assessment criteria from Part 1 yet? No? Then, I recommend you be willing to take the loss if cornered. Don't get pressured into marriage or moving in together when you know it is a mistake in your gut. Many men have made that mistake, hoping for the best, only to end up in misery. Don't let that be you.

**TIP 4:** I also recommend deciding what your policy is on major decision-making authority in your relationships. Some couples are fine with 50/50. I recommend considering having one person in charge and accountable for larger decisions, and I suggest that be you. I think that arrangement helps reduce the conflict and number of arguments in a relationship. For example, from my personal life, for most things it is 90/10, and she is the 90. I don't care about or want to know about most small details, but I do roughly want to know what is going on for budgeting reasons. For things I do care about, it is 60/40, and I am the 60. Being the 40 with guys like us is a very good thing. Having that 40% influence over decisions means she gets to express her input, and that is very carefully and thoughtfully heard, but once the discussion stops progressing, 60 makes the final decisions. If you are a non-50/50 person, you need to sort this out as a couple.

**TIP 5:** Finally, I find it worthwhile to mention again the importance of flirting—consider never stopping. Maybe make it a lifelong hobby, if only limited to your wife or girlfriend. As hobbies go, it isn't a bad one—making people happy and feel good about themselves.

I hope this book is helpful for you. As I type this, I am looking at a list of goals for this book that I taped on one of my monitors. Those goals include my desire for the book to be life-changing for you. They also include having at least one impactful idea or useful thing on every single page. No filler was allowed. I want this book to be the best money you have ever spent. I want this book to merit being on your list of favorite books of all time.

As you have seen, we went far past what the title of the book suggested. I felt that having the book truly deliver on the title's promise meant more than presenting you with a couple hundred pages of pickup lines. It required showing you how to be a confident person who draws people to you in all aspects of life, including women. It required laying out an effective plan to achieve your goal of finding a great woman. It required providing the conversation tools to help make a connection. It required giving you real-world advice to help you be successful through the process.

I wish you nothing but the best in life. Let's get to work! Let's go!

> Whatever you think you can do, or dream you can, begin it. Boldness has genius, power, and magic in it.
> JOHN ANSTER WITH INSPIRATION FROM JOHANN WOLFGANG VON GOETHE

# Part 5.
# TOOLS & LINKS

## Transition and Cute Expression Toolbox

The following table is a long series of interesting expressions that you can use to spice up the conversation in your dates and throughout the entire process. Consider these to be like small Lego blocks that you can put together in infinite ways. There are thousands of possibilities, we include quite a few here to get your creative juices flowing. I tried not to repeat anything from the conversation examples in Part 2 and 3.

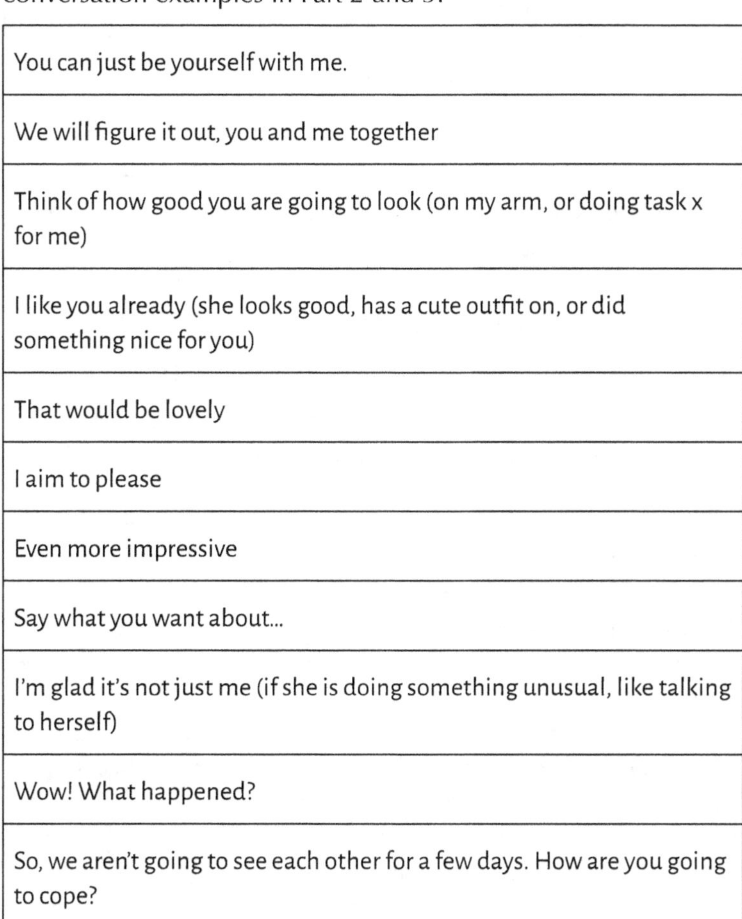

| You can just be yourself with me. |
| --- |
| We will figure it out, you and me together |
| Think of how good you are going to look (on my arm, or doing task x for me) |
| I like you already (she looks good, has a cute outfit on, or did something nice for you) |
| That would be lovely |
| I aim to please |
| Even more impressive |
| Say what you want about... |
| I'm glad it's not just me (if she is doing something unusual, like talking to herself) |
| Wow! What happened? |
| So, we aren't going to see each other for a few days. How are you going to cope? |

| |
|---|
| I'm not proud of that (referencing some shameful thing or act as joke and smiling) |
| Ahhh. You are so sweet! |
| How do you do that? That looks so good or looked seemingly effortless. |
| I love that you did that! |
| With your permission, I would like to... |
| If you will permit it, I would like to... |
| You aren't messing around, are you? (for when she just did something you thought was impressive or great) |
| You should follow me around, solving any problems that arise |
| You are the best! |
| You are funny, smart, and pretty in equal measure. You're something else—the whole package! |
| small price to pay |
| I know what you're thinking... |
| It's going to be so satisfying... |
| ... noted and logged for future reference ... (some idea, feedback or suggestion of hers that you cannot act on at the moment) |
| True, I have a bit of a crush on you |

| |
|---|
| I am not trying to pressure you |
| You will either love it or hate it. I am not sure there is an in-between for this one. |
| I've been teased, yet again. |
| In the words of William Shakespeare <a fake quote> |
| Thanks, I am glad you are seeing things my way. <smile> |
| Thousands of years of tradition |
| Critics are calling it the best/worst |
| Much better than the original |
| Let's raise the stakes even higher. |
| This is courting conversation gold! |
| There is more greatness to come! Why? There couldn't be less greatness after that last part. |
| Shock and awe |
| Are you all in? |
| This is a triumph of <something funny> |
| It is one of the perks of dating me. |
| Where is my cuddle? |

| This is an outrage! (joking tone) |
|---|
| She humbly says... |
| **Her:** Would you lie to me?<br><br>**You:** " Only if it was absolutely convenient". |
| **Her:** (laughs> Why are you picking on me?<br><br>**You:** <smile> Because it's fun! |
| **Her:** Never mind, I don't know what I am doing.<br><br>**You:** I don't know, but I do know that you look cute doing it. |
| **Her:** My friend thought you were great.<br><br>**You:** (boldly and smiling) Who wouldn't? |
| She flips you the bird playfully.<br><br>**You:** <smile> That's right, I'm number one. |
| Flirtatious? Me? What do you mean? |
| I can do better than this with the flirting. I'll step it up. (a flirting blooper, flubbed line, or other mishap) |
| In keeping with tradition... |
| "It's not my style to be so mysterious, but I cannot tell you about that right now". She is asking about your plans for the date, or some other surprise |

| You can just be yourself with me. |
|---|
| ... to really see someone ... meaning to get to know them at their core. |
| Every time I see you, you get prettier. How do you do it? |
| Are you impressed yet?" |
| Situational—If you or she trip over your own feet walking or do something else clumsy, recover with "we'll have that fixed immediately <smile>." |
| "May I" before a touch or something else where a gentleman might ask for her permission. For example, before taking her hand to lead her somewhere. |
| I love fresh vegetables. Don't even knock the dirt off mine. |
| **Her:** Are you for real?<br><br>**You:** I am the real deal. I have no time or energy for faking it or doing otherwise. I am serious about this and wouldn't waste your time, or mine, with any games or deception. |
| I think the standards have lowered a bit because... |
| **Her:** You're funny, a head full of jokes.<br><br>**You:** It's a jungle up there. |
| We are going to need some private time. (a very nice way to bring up the idea of intimacy) |
| First, I totally break it, then I fix it. (a small, seemingly simple task goes awry while she is looking) |

| Maybe that sounds better than what it is. |
|---|
| Upon closer inspection... |
| Missed good parking spot. You: "Oh me of little faith" |
| I want to take just a moment to enjoy (or savor) that joke. |
| It's just a fact |
| Your hero |
| Later, when the cameras were off... |
| I had dreamed of |
| I lie only if necessary, or convenient |
| You are my favorite you know that right |
| Everything about you is pretty. And I think you are interesting... |
| With all humility |
| Expert marksman! Can shoot foot from any angle |
| I don't have problems. I have situations that I thrive in. |
| I stand in awe |
| I love the sound of envy |
| It's music to my ears |

| No one is a bigger proponent of <insert funny or unexpected thing here> than me. |
|---|
| I think the real story here is that ... |
| You should follow me around all day solving all my problems |
| This food is manna from heaven compared to ... |
| Doctors should prescribe dating me to improve overall wellness. |
| So humble and lovable |
| Special hug |
| I am a model of impeccable behavior |
| Do you have any advice for me? |
| Here on humanitarian mission |
| What is a typical day in the life |
| Wow you are humble. Humble to the core. |
| Let's have a pre-date |
| Just for the record... |
| Feast your eyes |
| I'm awestruck |
| acclaimed |

| I have this near super-human ability |
|---|
| I'll indulge for the right price. |
| Let the picture paint itself |
| If I knew you better I would invite you |
| I don't know if it is genetics or something you were doing... |
| And I will tell you why... |
| This is the greatest moment in dating history |
| Overcome your skepticism |
| We share many of the same values |
| Some say one of the most important moments in a woman's life is when she... |
| I am the world's preeminent expert in... |
| The possibilities are limitless |
| I'd like to make an impression |
| Would it improve your opinion of me to know that I ... |
| Strut around like a peacock |
| World famous |
| You can thee the improvement |

| |
|---|
| Let's capture the moment by... |
| Unmatched quality |
| As a renowned expert in _____, I feel uniquely qualified to say... |
| We can only keep improving from here |
| You're halfway decent looking |
| "Heck yeah!" in response to a brag or boast |
| Don't accept anything less (or substitutes) |
| (smiling) Women from <her country, state or hometown's name> are notoriously <insulting term>.<br>*Example:* Women from Boston are notoriously/famously feisty/sassy. |
| It's like a love letter to you |
| You are about to trade up |
| When am I not thinking about... |
| You are about to get an upgrade |
| There she is in all of her manifest womanly glory! |
| I'll win you/her over |
| I'm the gold standard. Or, you're the gold standard. |
| Guilty as charged |

| |
|---|
| If you aren't thrilled with your options here, I can offer an upgrade (food, beverage, social scene, bar, etc) |
| You deserve it |
| Your principled approach |
| I like it when people feel like they owe me (smile) |
| The stakes couldn't be lower |
| Chock full of... |
| Consider words like captivating, stunning, and radiant instead of overusing pretty |
| This level of sex appeal |
| Am I not handsome enough? (joking tone) |
| I am sure you immediately recognized... |
| I don't have to tell you... |
| That's just the tip of the iceberg. |
| It only gets better from here. |
| It was all part of my plan. |
| If all else fails, consider an emoji. A winking one might work if she asked you something unanswerable. A smiling or laughing face are good, general purpose go-to moves as well. |

## TEN RULES

1. Be confident.
2. Have a plan. Always have something to say.
3. She needs to feel safe, comfortable, and unthreatened at all times.
4. Every interaction must be a positive experience for her throughout.
5. Don't be creepy.
6. Don't harass.
7. Never at your workplace or place of business.
8. Pre-screen and assess the situation and environment.
9. Smile and make eye contact.
10. Listen to her. Watch her body language.

## Useful Links

1. Help for creating your compatibility assessments is at *https://gentlemensguidetoflirting.com/assessment-creator.html*.
2. Any updates or corrections for this book will be announced on the podcast, social media, and *https://gentlemensguidetoflirting.com/*
3. The *Gentlemen's Guide to Flirting* podcast is available everywhere including Spotify and Apple Podcasts.
4. Leave me feedback at *https://twitter.com/guidetoflirting* or *https://www.instagram.com/gentsguidetoflirting/*.

Gather ye Rose-buds while ye may,
Old Time is still a-flying:
And this same flower that smiles to day,
To morrow will be dying.

The glorious Lamp of Heaven, the Sun,
The higher he's a getting;
The sooner will his Race be run,
And neerer he's to Setting.

That Age is best, which is the first,
When Youth and Blood are warmer;
But being spent, the worse, and worst
Times, still succeed the former.

Then be not coy, but use your time;
And while ye may, go marry:
For having lost but once your prime,
You may forever tarry.

HERRICK, ROBERT. "TO THE VIRGINS, TO MAKE MUCH OF TIME"
HESPERIDES, 1648, #208

www.ingramcontent.com/pod-product-compliance
Lightning Source LLC
Chambersburg PA
CBHW071806080526
44589CB00012B/707
*9781736798409*